THE FINANCIAL IMPACT OF CORPORATE EVENTS ON CORPORATE STAKEHOLDERS

The Financial Impact of Corporate Events on Corporate Stakeholders

SHARON H. GARRISON

Quorum Books
NEW YORK   WESTPORT, CONNECTICUT   LONDON

Library of Congress Cataloging-in-Publication Data

Garrison, Sharon Hatten.
    The financial impact of corporate events on corporate stakeholders
/ Sharon H. Garrison.
        p. cm.
    ISBN 0-89930-469-9 (lib. bdg. : alk. paper)
    1. Stocks—Prices. 2. Issues management. 3. Public relations—
Corporations. I. Title.
HG4636.G38   1990
332.63′222—dc20   90-8392

British Library Cataloguing in Publication Data is available.

Library of Congress Catalog Card Number: 90-8392
ISBN: 0-89930-469-9

First published in 1990

Quorum Books, 88 Post Road West, Westport, CT 06881
An imprint of Greenwood Publishing Group, Inc.

Printed in the United States of America

The paper used in this book complies with the
Permanent Paper Standard issued by the National
Information Standards Organization (Z39.48-1984).

10 9 8 7 6 5 4 3 2 1

Contents

Tables and Figures

Preface

The Bhopal disaster. The Tylenol murders. Ted Turner's attempted takeover of CBS. All news stories in recent years. All events that could affect the value of the company.

This book examines corporate events and their impact on stockholders. It explains the mechanisms of financial markets and how assets are valued. It examines sources of financial information and how that information is transmitted. It also shows how the impact of corporate events can be measured. Last, the book summarizes the findings of a number of academic research efforts on corporate events.

The Financial Impact of Corporate Events on Corporate Stakeholders is intended for anyone interested in such events. A reader need not be either a financial expert or an academic to learn from this book.

I am grateful to Michael Garrison, Nancy Hyder, and Shankar Char for their invaluable assistance in the preparation of this manuscript, as well as to Geri Hutchins, who helped prepare Chapter 4, and the *Journal of Financial and Strategic Decisions* for permission to use material.

THE FINANCIAL IMPACT OF CORPORATE EVENTS ON CORPORATE STAKEHOLDERS

Corporate Events: What They Are and How They Affect Owners

On Monday, December 3, 1985, the officers of Union Carbide Corporation woke to disaster. A pesticide plant in Bhopal, India, in which Union Carbide owned the majority interest, began leaking poisonous gas, and people were dying.

First reports were sketchy. Estimates of the death toll were initially placed at seventy-five. At first, the cause of the leak was purported to be sabotage. As more news filtered in, however, it became clear that initial reports were tragically underestimated. Soon it became apparent that this corporate event was one of the worst industrial accidents in history. By the time estimates of the tragedy were firmed up, over two thousand people were reported dead and tens of thousands were injured.

On Wall Street, traders clamored to unload Union Carbide stock. Within a short time the stock had plummeted by nearly a fourth of its previous value—from $48 to $37 a share. In the aggregate, that represented a loss of market value to shareholders of Union Carbide of about $900 million.

What caused such a drop? Quite simply, the traders in the stock market had assessed Union Carbide's future earnings potential after the disaster and decided that this potential was severely impaired.

For one thing, they anticipated the legal ramifications of the damage done by the leak. As soon as the gas cleared, lawyers were already lining up plaintiffs to seek billions of dollars in damages from Union Carbide. It was easy to envision suits being tied up in the courts for years, crippling Carbide's ability to make profits. Certainly, when settlements started being reached, Carbide's cash flow might be completely drained.

Another consideration was the safety of Carbide's other plants around the world and certainly in the United States. Fears that other problems would arise caused market traders to question Carbide's ability to earn profits from these ventures.

Yet another consideration was the lethal product itself, methyl isocyanate. A disaster such as Bhopal might cause health concerns about the product, which might eventually lead to curtailing its manufacture.

All of these factors would inevitably lead to the constriction of future cash flow and would therefore cause a loss in value of Union Carbide stock.

Another concern surfaced during the Bhopal tragedy, one that may have caused long-term concern about the future of Carbide. During the early stages of the incident, it became clear that Carbide officials had no disaster plan. In the days of heightened media coverage and instant transmission of information, this lack became media fodder. Because of this seeming lack of planning and lack of understanding of media impact, some investors lost confidence in Carbide management, affecting, therefore, the value of Carbide stock.

TYLENOL MURDERS

Johnson & Johnson also had a nightmare of historic proportions. In 1982, seven people in Chicago died after ingesting poisoned Tylenol capsules. At that time, Tylenol was Johnson & Johnson's chief product. A national panic ensued, and, understandably, the value of Johnson & Johnson's stock fell dramatically.

This case was markedly different from that of Union Carbide. First of all, it was clear from the outset that Johnson & Johnson had no responsibility for the Tylenol deaths. Perhaps the biggest difference was the way these disasters were handled by corporate officials. James

E. Burke was chair of Johnson & Johnson during this period, and if he did not have a disaster plan, he certainly acted as if he did.

Johnson & Johnson removed Tylenol capsules from the shelves immediately, a move many market analysts thought foretold financial disaster. The company then took immediate steps to promote tamper-proof packaging and started a skillful media campaign, which included addresses by Burke, news conferences, and an ad campaign built around the theme of trust. The downslide of Johnson & Johnson's sales turned around. This was one of the best examples in corporate history of good media relations. Certainly, Burke knew the power of information and media and won back the confidence of financial markets.

For a few years, Johnson & Johnson enjoyed steady growth, but in 1986 tragedy struck again. Although almost impossible to believe, Burke was back in front of the cameras after more tainted Tylenol was found, this time in New York. The impact the scare had on stock value was not so profound as in 1982, largely because of skillful media relations.

The Bhopal and Tylenol stories had some similarities, but one of the big differences between the two stories lies in the understanding of information and imagery.

E. F. HUTTON AND PLAYING THE FLOAT

Disaster struck E. F. Hutton on May 2, 1985, but it was a disaster of the company's own making. On that date Hutton admitted to an elaborate scheme of "playing the float." For some time, the company had been diverting money from one client account to another. It was reported that the company shuffled over $10 billion from one account to another, thereby obtaining the use of over $1 billion over a year and a half period.

The float was neither coincidental nor accidental. It was a sophisticated system designed to profit from check float, with full knowledge of company officials. On May 2, 1985, Hutton was cited on over two thousand counts of mail and wire fraud: It agreed to pay the maximum fine of $2 million to reimburse duped banks for lost interest and to pay $750,000 to defray government investigative costs.

The company's stock suffered a monumental loss, although the loss was not protracted. Long-term impact on the company may have led to its eventual acquisition in 1987.

CHRYSLER AND JEEP

Perhaps more than any other corporate leader in recent history, Lee Iacocca captured the interest and imagination of the American public. At the helm of Chrysler Corporation during its days of near-bankruptcy, he successfully steered the company out of troubled waters. His parade of successes was long. The government bail-out, the early pay-off of the loan, the huge Voyager-Caravan market—all made big news.

In 1987 Chrysler announced plans to acquire American Motors Corporation. The motives that spurred the purchase were mainly the acquisition of the popular Jeep and the market for the rugged utility vehicle. In addition, American Motors plants were operating at only 49 percent capacity; additional capacity attributable to the Jeep purchase would be cheaper for Chrysler than building new capacity for growth.

In the short run, the market viewed the acquisition favorably. The long-term verdict is still out, however.

CBS BUY-BACK

Some mergers are not friendly. Some do not work out, and many are the focus of media attention.

Ted Turner is no stranger to the media spotlight. A flamboyant sports figure and creator of a cable television empire, he was used to making news himself. When Turner attempted to take over CBS Incorporated in 1985, he was yet again the focus of media attention. For whatever reason, he attempted a hostile take-over of CBS. The plan would have cost Turner Broadcasting about five billion dollars, but the managers of CBS were appalled by the take-over attempt. Immediately after the take-over attempt became clear, legal maneuvering and name calling began. Eventually CBS thwarted Turner by buying up almost one million dollars of its own stock.

Who won? Probably nobody. Turner's legal fees most likely surpassed profits that he made on CBS stock, and CBS stock fell dramatically. The cash strain caused by the buy-back could affect CBS for some time. All in all, the values of both companies involved in the incident were diminished.

GENERAL MILLS SPINS OFF

Not all corporate news revolves around companies gobbling up one another. Sometimes corporations make news when they "spin off" or divest themselves of divisions or subsidiaries. In recent years, food companies have caught merger fever, but it is not the first time they have done so. Indeed in the early 1980s there was a wave of merger activity in the food industry. General Mills, like a number of others, succumbed to the fever.

After awakening, though, many of these companies were unhappy with diversification. General Mills was no exception. The company was used to being a winner. For 22 years, it had established a consistent pattern of earnings increases. That ended in 1984, even though earnings from food interests were up. Problems with Red Lobster restaurants, clothing company holdings, and toy company interests caused profits to decline nearly 5 percent.

There appeared to be no end in sight to the downward trend in profits. General Mills started thinking it couldn't stand the heat and perhaps should get back to the kitchen. To correct the situation, General Mills announced it was going to sell two of its three nonfood businesses—Izod, Parker Brothers, and Kenner Products.

Evidently the news was what the market wanted to hear, because the day after the announcement on January 28, 1985, the company's stock jumped about 10 percent (from 49⅜ to 55¼). A 10 percent increase in one day is remarkable in any sense.

CORPORATE EVENTS

Although different in nature, these events have something in common: they each affected the firm's stock price. For that reason, it might pay to know something about the nature of corporate events, how they might affect a firm's stock price, and when such an impact is felt.

Corporate events that might influence stock price include such things as mergers, industrial accidents, key executive changes, changes in debt ratings, proxy fights, dividend announcements, announcements of stock repurchases, and like events. Those who understand such events and how they influence stock prices may benefit positively.

Who Uses Information about Corporate Events?

Managers might use such knowledge in designing strategies. For example, if a company was contemplating the repurchase of common stock, it might be able to predict in advance how the repurchase might affect the market value of the stock and when. The company might also use such knowledge in determining how to structure the repurchase and could even figure out the best way to announce the repurchase to the media.

Managers might also use corporate event knowledge to aid in managing unexpected events. By understanding how information influences stock price behavior, managers might be able to soften the blow of unexpected corporate events and even avert disaster, such as Johnson & Johnson did. Managers, knowing how surprise events might affect investor perception, can plan for such eventualities. They may even train key employees in implementing a disaster plan.

Investors could use information about corporate events in molding investment strategies. There are a couple of things they should keep in mind. First, there is the short-term impact of corporate events, but perhaps there is also a longer-term impact. By watching how a management team handles corporate events, observers can judge the quality of management. In other words, does management understand the nature of the event and how and when it is felt in the market?

For instance, suppose a company is contemplating the take-over of another company. There of course will be a short-term impact on the stock of both companies as negotiations go forth. There is also a long-term impact to be determined by watching management perform its job. A hostile take-over may involve negative press, name calling, allegations of incompetence, and the like. Such actions must cast doubt on the quality of the management team. If negotiations proceed professionally, with a minimal amount of negative press, then an observer may conclude that the team "has its act together." In that case, the investor might conclude that such a progressive management might handle other events in a like manner. In fact, the management team might even bring the same degree of professionalism and skill to managing day-to-day events, which should result in profits. So, the skill of managers in handling corporate events can give investors clues about the abilities of managers over the long run as well as the short run.

Business researchers also need to understand how corporate events affect stock prices and ultimately stockholder wealth. This book contains the results of a vast number of research efforts concerning corporate events. It focuses not only on the events themselves, but on the transmission of information and techniques for measuring the impact of that information.

The key link between corporate events and stock price changes is information. In today's world information travels freely and quickly. The acquisition, transmission, and interpretation of information has become a huge enterprise around the globe. To compete in such an environment, it is necessary to understand how information is transmitted and how it affects security prices. The next chapters look at related topics.

REFERENCES

Kirkland, Richard I. "Union Carbide: Coping with Catastrophe." *Fortune,* January 7, 1985, pp. 51–53.

Nielsen, John. "Switching to Caplets." *Fortune,* March 17, 1986, pp. 44–49.

Wall Street Journal: March 10, 1987, p. 3 (Chrysler); March 21, 1985, p. 3 (Union Carbide); January 29, 1985, p. 2 (General Mills); October 1, 1982, p. 2 (Johnson & Johnson).

2

Markets and Value

The previous chapter explored some corporate events and alluded to the fact that such events might affect stock prices. To understand the intricacies of stock price behavior, it is first necessary to understand how markets function.

MARKET MECHANISMS

Maybe one of the best ways to visualize market transactions and mechanisms is to remember some of the old "B" adventure movies or serials. Oftentimes in such movies, the hero conducts a market transaction in an exotic bazaar. The seller extols the virtues of his merchandise—say, for instance, a camel. Perhaps he points out the excellence of the camel's blood lines, the perfect symmetry of its humps; perhaps he talks about how young the camel is, and insists that it hardly ever eats or drinks.

The interested buyer, however, pulls on his beard, eyes the camel with disdain, and does his best to disparage the animal. He calls it a veritable fleabag, purports that it is on its last legs, and probably isn't even good enough for dog food. Then the actual haggling over price begins. The buyer makes an insultingly low offer. The seller counters

Figure 2.1
Supply and Demand

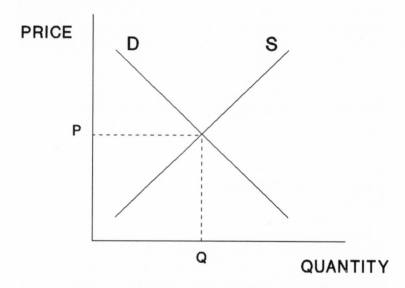

with high price equally ridiculous. The haggling goes back and forth for some time, until finally a deal is struck.

This, in its rawest form, is how a market functions. Buyers and sellers come together in the market. The forces of supply and demand meet, and the goods are finally sold at a fair price. This is the classic equilibrium notion of supply and demand as illustrated in Figure 2.1. These same forces exist in financial markets, where securities are traded. Although the goods traded are quite different—real goods as opposed to paper goods—the bazaar and financial market have a great deal in common.

FUNCTIONS OF A FINANCIAL MARKET

Although larger and more sophisticated, financial securities markets, such as organized stock exchanges and bond exchanges, operate in much the same fashion as the bazaar. Buyers and sellers of goods, in this case securities, come together, the forces of supply and demand interact, and the goods are sold at a fair price.

Why would someone buy a financial security, such as a share of stock in a company? It might be obvious why the buyer of the camel was interested. The camel provides basic personal transportation and company on long nights in the desert, and is probably capable of performing certain work. With this notion in mind, someone might query, "What good is a share of common stock?"

In essence, the value of the stock will derive from its cash flows—the cash the owner of that security can generate. The cash flows generated from holding a stock flow from two sources: dividends and appreciation in the stock's market price.

If a company makes a profit during a financial period, it may divide those profits among the owners of the company, plow them back into the company, or a combination of the two. Dividends are profits paid to the owners, and retained earnings are those plowed back into the company. The dividends paid represent cash flows to the individual owners of the firm's stock.

If someone purchases a share of stock in a company for $100 and sells it sometime later for $138, a positive cash flow of $38 is realized by the owner of that security. The stock has appreciated in market price.

The reason stocks appreciate in price is perhaps not so obvious. The reason hearkens back to market processes. Buyers and sellers of common stock come together in a financial market. They haggle over goods and, in doing so, force goods to be sold at fair prices. A price change, then, represents a change in the consensus of this market process. Something has caused the market to change its opinion of the underlying value of the good being traded.

When someone buys a share of stock in a company, they are paying to become an owner in that company. When stock is traded in the market, the trades represent changes in ownership—just as the camel was exchanged from the seller in the bazaar to the buyer. The buyer of the camel was willing to pay a price in order to obtain transportation, company, a work animal, or something of that nature. In other words, the value of that transportation, company, or whatever was reflected in the final price.

In the long run, stock price changes represent changes in market consensus about the value of ownership in a company. The only thing that will cause a fundamental change in stock price is a change in the anticipated future earnings of the company, because the only reason someone would pay to become an owner in a company is to share in its future expected profits. In other words, in the long run, anticipated profits are the primary determinant of value of the company, and therefore stock price.

There are also short-term aberrations that affect stock prices as a matter of course, some of which will be addressed later in this book.

INFORMATION AND MARKET FORCES

If one of the participants in a market transaction has access to information that another does not, then an imbalance may occur. For instance, assume that the seller of the camel knows that it has a congenital degenerative disease. Although the camel now looks healthy, the owner knows that within the next year the camel will most likely fall ill and die, which certainly affects its value. The buyer, without access to such information, will probably pay too high a price.

On the other hand, if the buyer had observed the camel swallow a diamond that some jewel thief had dropped the day before, and discovered that the owner did not know of this fortunate circumstance, then the buyer may be at an unfair advantage. The owner then may sell the camel for too low a price.

In either case, this limited access to information caused an imbalance in market forces; in both cases the price reached was not a fair price for the good being traded.

More than likely, such imbalances were not infrequent in the camel market. The nature of the market probably dictates that such imbalances will occur from time to time. Financial markets, on the other hand, may or may not be subject to these same flaws. If information is not available to all the participants in the financial markets, then such market imbalances may occur. If they do, the market is said to be inefficient. If they do not, the market is said to be efficient.

MARKET EFFICIENCY

Market efficiency is a difficult notion. Perhaps the best explanation is to contrast an inefficient market with an efficient one. The market for real estate is generally regarded as inefficient, and the organized stock exchanges, such as the New York Stock Exchange, is regarded as efficient. The term "inefficient" does not imply anything derogatory; it simply describes how the market functions.

Inefficient Markets

Jim and Beverly bought their first home eight years ago. At that time it was the perfect home—the right size for the right price. They paid $75,000 and felt the price was a bargain. Now, eight years and three kids later, they realized they have outgrown their home and feel it is time to move up.

They decide to sell, but they must make one important decision—the price they want for the house. They realize this is a pretty tough decision. They at first think they should start from the $75,000 base price they paid for the house, then quickly realize that this line of thinking is naive. Housing prices have gone up a lot in the past eight years. Not only that, there are a lot of regional variations in prices. They couldn't just figure a 12 percent increase per year and be done with it.

They next research what other houses in the neighborhood have sold for recently. After Beverly contacts several neighbors, however, she finds that no house in the neighborhood has been sold in the past three years.

They contact a realtor and ask for help. The realtor says $157,000 might be a ballpark figure, but refuses to advise them further. Jim and Beverly ask if the multiple listing book can help them, but are told that the book only gives asking prices and not actual selling prices.

A friend of Jim's advises them to check the courthouse records and see if any deeds have been recorded for comparable homes. Unfortunately, most list as transaction price "ten dollars and other good and valuable considerations."

In exasperation Jim yells, "Why isn't there a book that lists different kinds of houses in different kinds of neighborhoods and the prices they should sell for?" Jim probably won't find a book like that, because he has run up against one of the characteristics of an inefficient market—the relative lack of information.

Dave and Janet were in the same situation. They were thinking of selling their home and tried to decide on a price. They lived next door to a home that was similar to theirs, and it went up for sale in October. In January it was sold to a couple from New Jersey. Three months later, the couple moved in. Dave and Janet got to know them and finally felt comfortable enough to ask what they had paid for the house. This illustrates the second characteristic of an inefficient market—what little information is available is transmitted slowly. This relatively slow transmission of information characterizes the real estate market as well as other inefficient markets.

Dave and Janet and Jim and Beverly had another problem. It had been a long time since either couple had been involved in the real estate market, and they had all forgotten everything they knew about it. They had to relearn about escrow, closing costs, deeds of trust, and such matters. They felt this lack of knowledge put them at a disadvantage in negotiations. This relative lack of sophistication about market mechanisms on the part of some participants is another characteristic of inefficient markets.

Because of these factors, imbalances may occur. Tricia and Bill moved from Connecticut to Brownsville, Texas. They looked at a three-bedroom brick house for $138,600 and snatched it up before looking at another thing. Thinking of housing prices back in Connecticut, they thought they had a bargain. They didn't realize that they paid about 30 percent too much for the house. These market imbalances are characteristic of inefficient markets.

Something else may happen in an inefficient market that will result in market imbalances: not all investors look at transactions and underlying values in the same fashion. Pete and Nancy found out there were plans by the state to build a big freeway near their house, and they decided to sell quickly. They thought the noise from the freeway would be deafening, and that the value of their home would be drastically reduced.

Later Pete and Nancy discovered that all their former neighbors sold their homes for four times the prefreeway value to a developer who wanted to build a shopping center. This points out another characteristic of an inefficient market: participants do not always act rationally, at least according to experts in that market. The result is that goods traded in this market will not always trade at what would be considered a fair price—a price reflective of the true, underlying, inherent value of the goods.

Therefore, the real estate market is generally considered to be inefficient. These characteristics sharply contrast with those of the New York Stock Exchange.

Efficient Markets

The New York Stock Exchange is generally considered to be an efficient market. The idea of efficiency centers around information. Unlike the real estate market, there is an abundance of information available about the goods being traded on the stock exchanges. The companies whose securities are traded on the exchanges are required to furnish annual reports to shareholders, 10-k's and other forms to the Securities and Exchange Commission, and other information to exchange authorities. There are investment analysis services, such as Moody's, Standard and Poor's *Value Line Investment Advisory Services,* and a host of others, that analyze the stocks of companies traded on exchanges. There are on-line services where information can be transmitted from computer to computer. There are news stories in print media and electronic media. In fact, the amount of information available about the securities traded in this market is awesome. Perhaps the biggest problem a researcher would have is trying to figure out where to start.

The second point of contrast with the real estate market involves the speed of information transmission. Where the transmission of information in the real estate market is relatively slow, in the stock market it is almost instantaneous. As soon as some piece of information affecting the value of securities becomes available, it spreads at a blinding rate. Research has time and again illustrated how quick this transmission is. If a broker calls up and says he or she has a hot tip, it's probably not. Every trader between here and Wall Street probably already knows any news of substance.

Most traders in financial securities are in the market on an on-going basis. It is reasonable to assume they have built up some degree of sophistication about market mechanisms, which is in contrast to the way real estate and other inefficient markets function. If that is the case, and if investors in securities are rational, then it is assumed that traders use information in a rational manner. In other words, traders will use available information to see how underlying values of securities would be affected by it, and will buy or sell securities based on that concept of value. Participants in the market view the valuation process in the same manner. Following that line of reasoning, market imbalances should therefore not occur as they might in an inefficient market.

Table 2.1
Contrast: Efficient and Inefficient Markets

Inefficient Market	Efficient Market
Relative Lack of Information	Wealth of Information
Slow Transmision of Information	Rapid Transmission
Lack of Sophistication	Traders Sophisticated
Market Imbalances	Goods Traded for Fair Price
Participants May Be Irrational	Rational Traders

Whether all investors in a market act rationally might be subject to question. However, if a sufficient number of traders are rational, the forces of supply and demand will dictate that actions of irrational participants will be offset and that goods should trade at a price reflecting their inherent value.

The notion of efficiency, then, really centers around information— its availability, speed of transmission, and use by traders. Table 2.1 summarizes points of contrast between inefficient and efficient markets. If markets are efficient, there are certain implications for their participants.

Implications of Efficient Markets

If markets are efficient, then the price for which a good trades in that market is the inherent value of that security. It is also a price reflecting the publicly available information concerning that good. When new information about a good becomes available, it is disseminated quickly and prices react quickly. If all, or at least a sufficient number of, participants in a market have access to the same information and act on that information in the same fashion, then it follows that rarely would someone be able to "beat the market." In other words, in an efficient market a trader will not be able to make superior profits consistently.

That is not to say that someone cannot make a profit in the stock market. Investors can make profits; they will just not be able to consistently beat the average returns for average investors in that market.

This is also not to say that every once in a while someone won't get lucky and make a killing. It happens all the time. However, a trader will not be able to beat the market consistently. For that to happen, someone would have to have access to information other traders do not have (an unlikely circumstance for most investors), or someone would have to use that information in a manner other traders do not. In other words, someone would have to have a system. That too is also unlikely. With all the traders in the world, all the information, all the computers and other technological aids to analysis, it is difficult to believe that some new system could be devised that someone has not already tried.

Those are the implications of efficient markets. The next question then is: Are financial markets efficient?

The Efficiency of Financial Markets

Economic and financial thinkers come up with theories and hypotheses all the time. In testing all these ideas, research results are usually mixed. In many cases these ideas cannot get full support from the economic community, which is perhaps one reason why average citizens are often confused by economic commentators and their conflicting ideas about the state of the economy.

The theory that financial markets are efficient is an exception. There is a wealth of research supporting the assertion that U.S. financial markets are efficient; probably there is more support for efficient financial markets than any other economic theory to date.

The degree to which financial markets are efficient, however, is not agreed upon so unanimously. Some economists think the market is so efficient that even possessors of inside information cannot make superior profits. This thinking is probably naive, however. Anyone subscribing to it must not have ever read of the exploits of the likes of Ivan Boesky. Good insider information, although fraught with legal and ethical considerations, could probably yield its possessor superior profits.

Other economic researchers believe that insider information might indeed lead to superior profits, but they also believe the financial markets are efficient the rest of the time. Not too many other economists questioned this belief, at least not until October 19, 1987.

THE CRASH OF 1987

On Monday, October 19, 1987, financial history was made. Stock market losses for that one day were unprecedented. The markets were already jittery before trading opened that day. The previous Friday the Dow Jones Industrial Average had dropped more than 100 points. Financial markets in the Orient portended gloom for trading on Wall Street Monday morning. It turned out that everyone's worst fears were to come true.

The market opened at 9:30 A.M., and at first count the Dow was already down 67 points. Immediately the tide of trading threatened to suck everyone down. From the opening bell the smell of panic was in the air. Even television viewers watching network news reports or those following trades on the news networks knew that history was going to be made—and black history at that. After an hour of trading the Dow had fallen more than 100 points. In little more than one and a half hours, it was down more than 200 points. The sickening spiral continued throughout the day. Even after trading closed, exchange authorities continued to process paperwork for hours. The final tally showed that the Dow had slid 508 points.

News media heralded the loss as reminiscent of the market crash of 1929, and a general sense of foreboding set in.

All the rest of that week, prices in world markets bounced back and forth. Finally, when things settled a bit, analysts and economists started damage assessment and more than a few tried to figure out what had happened.

Some analysts called the drop a correction. Some said the market was signalling the beginning of a depression. Some blamed computerized trading, others blamed market manipulators. Most everyone said that panic selling was responsible for the magnitude of the losses.

No matter what everyone said, and no matter what the real cause of the crash was, it proved one thing: markets are not always totally efficient. It may have been before the crash, during the crash, or right after the crash, but the market had to be inefficient somewhere along the line. Financial markets are not always efficient, but they are most of the time. It is necessary to next explore the nature of financial information and how it affects value.

REFERENCES

Banz, R. W. "The Relationship between Return and Market Value of Common Stocks." *Journal of Financial Economics* (March 1981): 3–18.

Black, F., Jensen, M., and Scholes, M. *Studies in the Theory of Capital Markets.* New York: Praeger, 1972.

Brown, Stewart. "Earnings Changes, Stock Prices, and Market Efficiency." *Journal of Finance* (March 1978): 17–28.

Fama, Eugene. "The Behavior of Stock Market Prices." *Journal of Business* (January 1965): 34–105.

———. "Efficient Capital Markets: A Review of Theory and Empirical Work." *Journal of Finance* (May 1970): 383–417.

Gordon, Myron. *The Investment Financing and Valuation of the Corporation.* Homewood, Ill.: Irwin Publishing, 1962.

Hicks, J. R. *Value and Capital,* 2d ed. Oxford: Clarendon Press, 1946.

Kellison, S. G. *The Theory of Interest.* Homewood, Ill.: Irwin Publishing, 1970.

3

Concepts of Value and Risk and Return

The value of a good is what it is worth to someone, and that is a nebulous concept. For instance, a master painting may be just a picture to some, but priceless to others. A family heirloom of precious metal might be melted down for the value of materials, but it may also carry a sentimental value. Certainly, there are a number of emotional factors, difficult to measure, in valuing items. A working definition of value might be the cash flows associated with holding an asset. That is a strictly quantitative definition, but may be easier to grasp than a qualitative one.

VALUATION OF CASH FLOWS

In strictly quantitative terms, the value of an asset will derive from the cash flows generated from holding that asset. Again, this definition of value does not take into account other benefits from holding an asset. Rather, this definition looks at only those benefits that can be easily measured. To reduce the process to a simple formula, the process of valuation might appear:

$$V_0 = \frac{CF_1}{(1+r)^1} + \frac{CF_2}{(1+r)^2} \cdots \frac{CF_n}{(1+r)^n}$$

where

V_0 = value of an asset at time period 0

CF_1 = cash flows in year one

CF_2 = cash flows in year two

CF_n = cash flows in year n

r = required rate of return (or discount rate)

In other words, the value of an asset (therefore, the price one would be willing to pay for it) depends on the discounted value of all future cash flows over a holding period.

For an apartment building, the cash flows associated with holding that asset might be the net cash flows generated from the rental receipts on the building. For a bullion coin, such as a Krugerrand, the value would derive from the value of the metal contained in the coin. For a bond, the cash flows would arise from two sources: the interest payment on the bond and the maturity value. These cash flows are then compared to other bonds of similar quality available on the market. A preferred stock is valued based on its fixed and stated dividends until maturity.

Common stock is not so easy an asset to value, though. Theoretically, its value would derive from dividends paid on the stock and any appreciation in market value. Unlike dividends paid on preferred stock, the dividends on common stock are not fixed and stated. Common stock dividends are only paid when and if the board of directors of a corporation declare them. Even then it is difficult to value these dividends, because dividends may, and probably will, vary over time. Some corporations do not even pay dividends.

Then there is the appreciation in market price of the stock with which to contend in valuing the stock. The gain represents a positive cash flow to the owner of the stock and depends upon the market price of the stock at the end of some time period. Theoretically, that price will depend upon the market's assessment of future cash flows from the ownership of the stock, in other words, the value of all future dividends paid on the stock. With that notion in mind, a quantitative framework for valuing stocks might be derived as illustrated in appendix one to this chapter. For less intrepid readers the model is boiled down to the following:

$$P_0 = \frac{D_1}{r - G}$$

where

P_0 = Price of stock at time 0

D_1 = Expected dividends over the next year

r = Investors' required rate of return

G = Expected growth rate in dividends

In other words the price of a stock is the present value of all future dividends.

There are also problems with this framework, however. For instance, it is not a satisfactory method for valuing stock of companies that pay no dividends. Even companies that pay erratic dividends are not accurately covered by this model. There are a number of other problems with using this model in actual practice. It may serve as a guideline in investment decision making, but investors should also keep the earnings of the company in mind.

EARNINGS

As mentioned in the previous chapter, the reason someone would want to buy a share of stock in a company would be to become a part owner in that company, and therefore to share in profits. The present value of the market's estimate of the company's future profits, then, is the actual value of the stock in a company.

HOW TO ESTIMATE A VALUE

The valuing of stocks is obviously no easy matter. It involves analyzing some qualitative factors and tempering that information with quantitative analysis. Therefore, it may involve science as well as art. It may also be thought of as a "top-down" proposition, where an

Figure 3.1
Top-Down Forecast

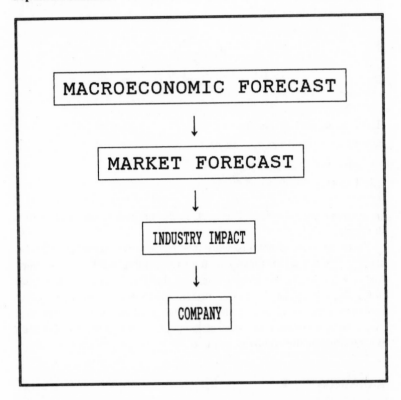

analyst looks at macroeconomic information, figures potential impact on financial markets, how such changes will affect the industry, then what will happen to the individual company given all these influences. The process is illustrated in Figure 3.1.

Market Analysis

To predict where the financial markets are headed over the short term, an investor may look at economic indicators, money supply data, or both. Economic indicators may be leading indicators, coincident indicators, and lagging indicators.

Figure 3.2
Business Cycles

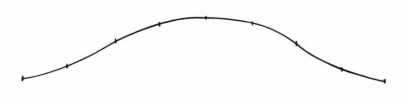

• At some point at the end of a recession, product demand starts to pick up.	• At some point, prices become too high.
• Increased demand causes increased sales.	• Demand slows down.
• To meet increased demand, employers increase labor force.	• General decrease in demand, sales, employment, money supply, prices and interest rates.
• Increased dollars cause increased money supply, interest rates and prices.	• Business cycle starts again.

Leading indicators are signals to the direction of future economic activity. Coincident indicators confirm the present direction of the market. Lagging indicators are variables that change after the direction of the business cycle changes. They confirm the stage of a business cycle. By analyzing such variables, someone may get a feel for the direction and stage of a business cycle. Figure 3.2 illustrates some of the things that happen during business cycles.

The National Bureau of Economic Research publishes economic indicators, and many are announced in federal reserve publications as well as in the popular media. Some variables that may be considered indicators are listed; some also include an explanation of why that variable may be a good indicator.

LEADING INDICATORS

- *Average Work Week of Production Workers.* If more workers are being hired back, and if such workers are working longer hours, this must be the result of plans by corporations to meet increased demand. The reverse is also true.
- *Index of New Business Formations.* If the outlook for the economy is generally good, then entrepreneurs and other investors will be willing to start businesses in order to partake in increased economic growth.
- *Index of Stock Prices*
- *Index of New Building Permits.* Construction activity tends to pick up when economic growth is expanding.
- *Layoff Rate.* If companies are expecting a downturn in economic activity, they tend to scale down, precipitating a reduction in labor force. The reverse is also true.
- *Money Supply*
- *Contracts and Orders of Plant and Equipment.* When companies expect an increase in economic activity and consequently demand, they will invest in productive facilities in order to meet that projected demand, and vice-versa.
- *Net Change in Inventory*
- *New Factory Orders*

COINCIDENT INDICATORS

- *Number of Nonagricultural Employees.* Once a business cycle change is in place, workers will be in the labor force keeping up with demand. The force should be static until anticipated changes occur.
- *Index of Industrial Production*
- *Manufacturing and Trade Sales*
- *Personal Income*

LAGGING INDICATORS

- *Average Duration of Employment.* This is an indication of turnover and normally lags behind business cycle changes.
- *Manufacturing and Trade Inventories*
- *Labor Cost Per Unit Output*

• *Average Prime Rate*

• *Commercial and Industrial Loans*

When assessing these indicators it is a good idea to look at the economic and statistical significance of each variable. Then a checklist of the indicators may be drawn. Not all of the indicators may be pointing in the same direction, but a feel for the direction is probably clear. For example, assume that the leading indicators check list appeared thus:

Average Work Week of Production Worker	↑
Index of New Business Formations	↑
Index of Stock Prices	↑
Index of New Building Permits	↑
Layoff Rate	↓
Money Supply	↑
Contracts and Orders for Plant and Equipment	↑
Net Change in Inventory	↓
New Factory Orders	↓

An experienced investment analyst with access to specialized tools would probably weigh these variables statistically and come up with a framework for predicting economic changes.

It is, however, still possible to get a feel for the future direction of the economy without some of these specialized tools. In assessing the above check list it is evident that the general trend of nearly all the variables is upward.

This is just a prediction of where the economy is moving, however. Other variables enter in to valuing a stock, such as how economic changes will affect the industry.

Industry Analysis

Industry factors will affect the value of common stocks. Important factors to consider are the stage of development of the industry, the nature of the industry product (e.g., low or high unit price, long or short life), industry capital situation, competitive factors, governmental regulation and control, shares of markets, and changes in market share in recent years. One of the most important factors is the historical industry growth relative to economic changes. When the industry analysis is complete, it is time to consider the individual company.

Company Analysis

The last tier on the analysis of a stock is the individual company analysis. Analysts approach this process in different ways. Many look at qualitative factors: They evaluate the management team, including a past history of successes and failures. Some may look at efficacy of cost controls, relations with labor, innovativeness in new products, and any competitive edge over other companies in the industry.

Some analysts look at quantitative factors: variations in prices of the company's stock, financial ratios, debt capacity, and the like.

Some assimilate both qualitative and quantitative factors in an overall evaluation of a company. Examples of many such approaches appear in Appendixes 3.1 and 3.2.

RISK

It is not enough to just look at returns. The added dimension of risk must be considered also. Risk does not necessarily mean something bad. Risk, in a financial sense, just means surprise. Clearly, there are other kinds of risks, but just as with returns, investors more than likely look at quantitative rather than qualitative aspects of investing.

Ideas about the riskiness of different kinds of securities are probably formed by looking at past price history. The more surprises in a company's past, the more risk an investor will perceive. Several aspects of risk might be considered. These aspects involve some statistical precepts; however, there is nothing in these next passages that should confound even a novice to statistics.

HOLDING PERIOD RETURNS

Before going much further it is necessary to examine the structure for calculating holding period returns from owning a stock. From the previous discussion, it was shown that cash flows from common stocks arise from two sources: appreciation/depreciation in market price and dividends.

To calculate holding period returns, the dividends received over one year, added to the gain or loss for each share of stock for that year, will be divided by the stock's price at the beginning of the year. For instance, assume XYZ stock was $58 on the first day of the year. During that year the company paid dividends totalling $3, and the price of the stock at the end of the year was $65. That works out to dividends of $3 added to market appreciation of $7 ($65 − $58)—a total gain of $10. That, divided by the original price, will give 17.24 percent.

Now assume that DEF stock lost value. The price of DEF at the beginning of the year was $65, but the price at the end of the year was only $55. The stock paid a $2 dividend over that year. The $2 dividend will offset some of the $10 depreciation in market price ($55 − $65), for a net loss of $8 ($2 − $10). That negative $8, divided by the beginning price of $65, yields a negative holding period rate of return of 12.31 percent.

A formula for calculating holding period rates of return might appear as:

$$HPR = \frac{D_1 + (P_1 - P_0)}{P_0}$$

where

HPR = Holding period rate of return

D_1 = Dividends over year

P_1 = Market price per share at end of year

P_0 = Market price per share at beginning of year

For instance, assume the following dividend and price schedule for Global stock is available:

GLOBAL STOCK

Year	Dividend	Price—End of Year
1987		$30
1988	$1.13	27
1989	1.15	28
1990	1.17	30
1991	1.19	31

The holding period return for 1988 would be calculated by plugging numbers into the HPR formula:

$$\text{HPR (88)} = \frac{1.13 + (27 - 30)}{30}$$

$$= -6.23\%$$

In other words, even though a dividend was paid on Global stock in 1988, there was a negative holding period rate of return because of the decline in stock price.

Holding period rates of return for Global stock for remaining years are calculated:

$$\text{HPR (89)} = \frac{1.15 + (28 - 27)}{27}$$

$$= 7.96\%$$

$$\text{HPR (90)} = \frac{1.17 + (30 - 28)}{28}$$

$$= 11.32\%$$

$$\text{HPR (91)} = \frac{1.19 + (31 - 30)}{30}$$

$$= 7.30\%$$

It is not enough to make investment decisions based upon returns alone, however. Risk must be taken into account. Now the job is to link returns with risk, starting with probability.

PROBABILITY

Probability is defined as the odds that some event will occur, based upon past history. For instance, assume someone added up the number of quarters of economic data over the past 25 years. There would of course be 100 quarters. Then suppose they added up the number of quarters of boom periods and found there were 13. It might then be said that boom periods occurred 13 percent of the time (13/100). This is the "probability" that a boom period will occur during the next period.

If that same person added up the so-called "normal" periods and found that there were 62, then the probability of a normal period is 62 percent (62/100). According to the classification scheme used for this data, there is only one state left—recession. (Obviously, there are actually many more states of the economy. Only three are used in this example for simplicity.)

If the only classification left is recession, then the probability must be 25 percent (100 − 13 − 62). So a probability distribution might appear as:

State of Occurrence	Probability State Will Occur
Boom	13%
Normal	62
Recession	25

EXPECTED RETURN

Expected return links the notions of return and probability. By multiplying outcomes under various states by the probability that the state will occur and aggregating results, an expected return is calculated.

For example, holding period rates of return based on past price history for XYZ and DEF companies are calculated. Then, holding period rates of return are averaged for each company under the various states of the economy. Results look like this:

	XYZ	DEF
Boom	50.00%	78.50%
Normal	30.00	30.00
Recession	5.00	−9.80

To calculate the expected return for each company, probabilities are multiplied by outcome then summed. For instance, for XYZ the expected return is calculated:

EXPECTED RETURNS FOR XYZ COMPANY

State	Probability	X	Outcome	=	
Boom	.13	x	.50	=	.0650
Normal	.62	x	.30	=	.1860
Recession	.25	x	.05	=	.0125

Expected Return   .2635

The expected return for DEF is calculated in

$$ER = \sum_{t=1}^{n} 0_1 \times Pr_1$$

where

ER = Expected return
O_1 = Outcome under various states
Pr_1 = Probability state will occur

EXPECTED RETURNS FOR DEF COMPANY

State	Probability	X	Outcome	=	
Boom	.13	x	.785	=	.1020
Normal	.62	x	.30	=	.1860
Recession	.25	x	-.098	=	-.0245

Expected Return   .2635

The expected return for each company is 26.35 percent. If an investor were to make decisions based on expected returns alone, XYZ and DEF are equally likely choices. DEF is clearly more troubling to a potential investor, however. Although returns are higher in boom pe-

Figure 3.3
Probability Graph: DEF

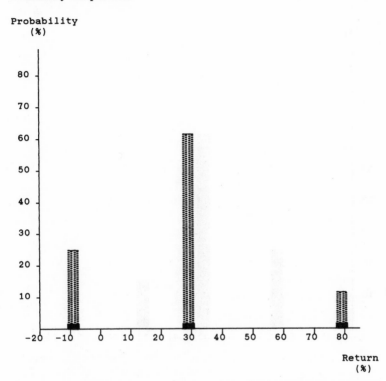

riods, an investor could lose money in recessions with DEF. In other words, an investor could have more surprises with DEF, and surprise is risk.

PROBABILITY GRAPH

A probability graph can be drawn to illustrate the riskiness of DEF compared to XYZ. Probabilities that a state will occur are shown on one axis, and returns given that state appear on the other. Figures 3.3 and 3.4 show probability graphs for DEF and XYZ. Figure 3.5 shows the results superimposed on one another. The primary note of interest in Figure 3.5 is that the results for XYZ are tighter, and those for DEF more dispersed. That dispersion is risk—deviation from the expected.

Figure 3.4
Probability Graph: XYZ

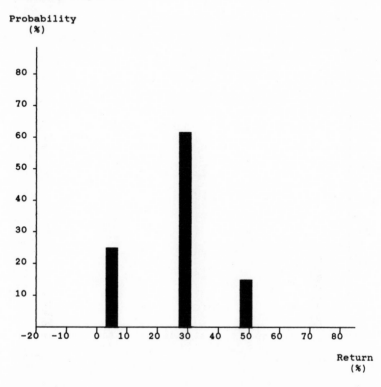

These results merely confirm what was already known: DEF is riskier than XYZ.

STANDARD DEVIATION

Another measure of risk is the standard deviation of returns. This measure shows how outcomes are dispersed about the mean. As in the probability graph, dispersion is risk—deviation from the expected.

To find standard deviations, the expected return (previous calculations already illustrated) is subtracted from the outcome under each state. This gives deviation about the mean, which is squared, then multiplied by the probability the state will occur. All results are then

Figure 3.5
Probability Graph: DEF and XYZ

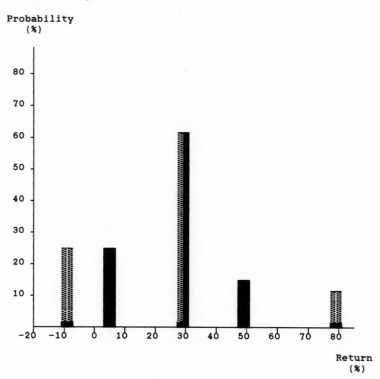

Probability
  (%)

Return
 (%)

summed. The sum is known as the variance of returns, which in itself is a widely accepted measure of risk.

The standard deviation of returns is simply the square root of the variance. The standard deviation for DEF and XYZ are shown in Tables 3.1 and 3.2. Again, DEF is riskier than XYZ.

The standard deviation of returns has a couple of useful properties. First, it is in the same units as are denominated returns. In other words, if the outcomes under each state are in dollars, the standard deviation will be in dollars. If returns are in percentages, the standard deviation will be in percentages.

Another useful property of standard deviation is that it gives a feeling for the potential outcomes of different investment alternatives. Most of the time (about 68 percent), outcomes will fall within plus or minus

Table 3.1

Standard Deviation of XYZ Company

```
Stage 1:
  Outcome - Expected Return = Deviation
  OC      - ER              = DV

Stage 2:
  (Deviation) × Probability = Variance
  (DV)        × PB          = VR
```

	Stage 1			Stage 2		
STATE	OC -	ER	= DV	(DV) ×	PB =	VR
Boom	.50 -	.2635	= .2365	.0559 ×	.13 =	.0073
Normal	.30 -	.2635	= .0365	.0013 ×.	.62 =	.0008
Recession	.05 -	.2635	= -.2135	.0456 ×	.25 =	.0114

Variance = .0195

Standard Deviation = $\sqrt{\text{Variance}}$ = .1396

one standard deviation of the expected return. So then, for DEF plus one standard deviation would be 52.59 percent (26.35 + 26.24) and minus one standard deviation would be .11 percent (26.35 − 26.24).

For XYZ plus one standard deviation would be 40.31 percent (26.35 + 13.96) and minus one standard deviation would 12.39 percent (26.35 − 13.96). See Figure 3.6 for an illustration of this notion. (About 95 percent of the time outcomes will be within plus or minus two standard deviations of the expected return.)

In analyzing XYZ and DEF, it is again evident that the range of outcomes for XYZ is a lot tighter. An observer would not be surprised to see outcomes of 3 percent and 50 percent for DEF, but that observer would certainly be surprised to see those outcomes for XYZ. In this sense, then, standard deviation is a good measure of risk.

SAMPLE DATA

The previous examples involved calculating returns and risk where there was a known probability distribution. If a known distribution is

Table 3.2
Standard Deviation of DEF Company

```
Stage 1:
  Outcome - Expected Return = Deviation
  OC      - ER              = DV

Stage 2:
  (Deviation) × Probability = Variance
  (DV)        × PB          = VR
```

STATE	Stage 1				Stage 2			
	OC	−	ER	=	DV	(DV)	× PB =	VR
Boom	.785	−	.2635	=	.5215	.2720	× .13 =	.0354
Normal	.300	−	.2635	=	.0365	.0013	× .62 =	.0008
Recession	−.098	−	.2635	=	−.3615	.1307	× .25 =	.0327

Variance = .0689

Standard Deviation = $\sqrt{\text{Variance}}$ = .2624

not available, then the best an investor can do is come up with an average rate of return and an estimate of the standard deviation. Assume some sample data for GHI company is available, as illustrated:

GHI COMPANY

Year	Holding Period Rate of Return
1986	5%
1987	−10
1988	15
1989	−5
1990	30
1991	10

To calculate average returns, the procedure is to simply sum outcomes for each year, and divide by the total number of years.

Figure 3.6
Relative Outcomes (About 68 percent of the time outcomes will fall within ±1 standard deviation of the expected return.)

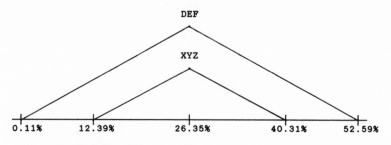

$(5-10+15-5+30+10$ or 45; that divided by 6 gives an average return of 7.5 percent).

To calculate the estimate of standard deviation the following formula may be used:

$$ES = \sqrt{\frac{\sum_{i=1}^{n}(O_1 - ARR)^2}{n-1}}$$

where

ES = Estimated standard deviation

O_1 = Outcome for each observation

ARR = Average rate of return

n = Number of observations

The formula simply implies that the average rate of return is subtracted from each observation to yield a deviation about the average return. This deviation is then squared. The results are summed, then divided by n − 1 observations. The square root of this number is then derived, and this represents the sample standard deviation. The sample standard deviation for GHI is 14.4 percent, as illustrated:

STANDARD DEVIATION GHI COMPANY

Observation	- Average	= Deviation	Squared Deviation
5	- 7.5	-2.5	6.25
-10	- 7.5	-17.5	306.25
15	- 7.5	7.5	56.25
-5	- 7.5	-12.5	156.25
30	- 7.5	22.5	506.25
10	- 7.5	2.5	6.25
			1037.50

1037.5 / 5 = 207.5

square root of 207.5 = 14.4

RETURNS VERSUS THE MARKET

The returns on individual securities may be compared to returns on the market in general. For instance, consider returns for GHI as previously shown, and returns for the whole market for the same years as shown below.

Year	GHI Returns	Returns on Market
1986	5%	6
1987	-10	-8
1988	15	17
1989	-5	-5
1990	30	25
1991	10	8

Figure 3.7
Equation of Regression Line

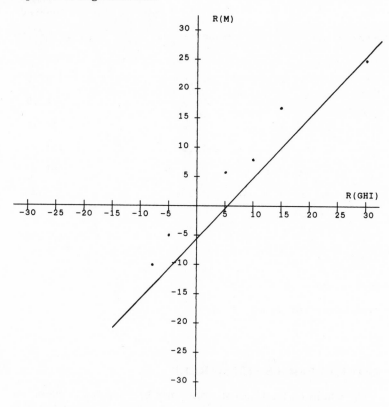

These returns may be plotted against each other as illustrated in Figure 3.7. An equation for the line may be derived using the form

$$r_x = a + b(r_m) + e$$

where

r_x = rate of return on an individual stock x

a = alpha intercept

b = slope of line

r_m = rate of return on the market

e = error coefficient

The alpha intercept for stock GHI is -5.9 percent. This beta is 1.13. So if the market were predicted to have a 12 percent return, GHI would be predicted to have a 7.7 percent return. Predicted returns for individual stocks may be calculated using this approach. This model, which can prove quite useful, is integral to the framework described in Chapter 5.

Appendix 3.1: Betas

As has been discussed, betas illustrate the relationship between rates of return on an individual security and rates of return on the market. With that in mind, some interesting inferences may be drawn regarding betas.

Betas are often used in investment analysis, but there are pitfalls and shortcomings, however. It is necessary to explore the notion of betas, how they may be used, and cautions regarding their use in investment analysis.

CLASSIFICATION OF BETAS

Betas show the relationship of rates of return on an individual security to the rate of return on the market as a whole. With that in mind there are certain classifications of betas that may be drawn. Table 3.3 illustrates the different classifications of ratios.

Beta of One

The stock of a firm may have a beta equal to one or close to one, indicating that its returns move fairly closely with the market. In the past, when the market was up, the stock of the company in question

Table 3.3
Classifications of Betas

BETAS	DESCRIPTION	TYPE OF COMPANY
Greater Than One	Stock Price Moves in Same Direction, But More Quickly Than Market	Volatile
Less Than One	Stock Moves Less Quickly Than Market	Defensive
Equal To One	Stock Moves With Market	Cyclical

also tended to be up, and to the same degree. The converse was also true. When the market was down, the rates of return on the individual stock were down to the same degree.

Stocks that tend to move with the market are known as cyclical stocks. These stocks change with the business cycle. A good example of cyclical companies is the automobile manufacturer. When the business cycle booms, individuals tend to have more discretionary income at their disposal, and they tend to spend it. Americans are known for their love of automobiles, so when they have the bucks they like to spend some on cars. When auto sales go up, the profits of automobile manufacturers go up, and consequently so do the returns on automobile company stocks.

On the other hand, when the business cycle is off, people may be out of work and, at the same time, individual salaries may be down, all of which results in less discretionary income. With fewer dollars at their disposal, individuals may have to cancel plans to replace their cars. Sales, earnings, and, consequently, stock returns for auto manufacturers will be down. So, when the business cycle changes, it is likely that automobile manufacturers' stock returns will likewise change.

Beta Less than One

A company may have a beta less than one, sometimes much less than one, meaning that the company's stock returns do not closely track changes in market returns. When the market is down, the returns of such companies may not be off to so great a degree, and vice-versa. The closer the beta to zero, the less relation there is to market returns.

When the market is up, the returns of these individual stocks may not increase to so great a degree. That does not mean that the rates of return for these individual companies do not vary. Indeed, earnings do fluctuate. Rather, a beta less than one means that the rates of return on individual stocks do not respond so greatly to the same variables that affect market returns.

Some analysts refer to stocks with betas less than one as defensive stocks, probably referring to the notion that returns on such stocks "defend" against changes in the business cycle. Again, returns on such stocks do vary, but in response to some reason other than pocketbook reasons, i.e., changes in discretionary income and the like.

Tobacco firms are good examples of defensive companies. People tend to be addicted to smoking. If the business cycle is off and discretionary income is cut, smokers may not be able to kick their habits. Therefore, dips in the business cycle will not necessarily result in decreased sales for tobacco companies. Conversely, if the business cycle is on an upswing and discretionary income jumps, that does not necessarily mean that smokers will all of a sudden smoke two packs of cigarettes a day instead of one. Obviously, the returns on tobacco stocks are not closely tied to changes in the business cycle or market returns. Returns on these individual stocks will more likely vary in response to people's health concerns.

Betas Greater than One

If the beta for a stock is greater than one, that means stock returns for that company move in the same direction, but to a much greater degree. When the market is up, the returns for such stocks are way up. When the market is down, the returns go way down. The rates of return for these companies are more volatile than those for average stock. The greater the beta, the greater the volatility.

For this book, a number of betas were calculated:

Company	Beta
IBM	1.05
Campbell Soup	.35
Federal Express	1.45

Some interesting insights may be drawn by analyzing these betas. For instance, IBM has a beta of 1.05, which would indicate that IBM stock in the past has pretty much moved with the market. Upon consideration, this makes sense. IBM's main line of business is office equipment and computers. When the business cycle is in an upswing, business activity is up, and businesses need equipment to keep up with all that activity. If these businesses are buying equipment from IBM, then IBM's revenues, profits, and stock prices will move up right along with the business cycle.

On the other hand, if the business cycle is heading downward, businesses realize they will face declines in sales and therefore tend to constrict cash flows. Any plans for office modernization or expansion are delayed or canceled. IBM's revenues, profits, and stock returns will decline.

Campbell Soup has a beta of .35, indicating that it is a defensive company. In other words, people tend to buy soup for reasons other than pocketbook reasons. People buy soup because they want to eat something light, because they want something warm on cold days, or any number of like reasons. Most of these reasons have little to do with changes in the business cycle, however. When the cycle and discretionary income are up, individual consumers are probably not going to rush out and buy two hundred cans of chicken noodle soup just because they have more cash available. Likewise, if income is off, people are probably still going to purchase soup, a can of which may cost around fifty cents. Therefore, soup sales and profits will not be affected by the fluctuations of the business cycle. Again, that is not to say the profits of Campbell Soup do not fluctuate—they do. Sales and profits will be affected by variables other than market variables, however.

Federal Express has a beta of 1.45, indicating that it is more volatile than the average stock on the market. Upon consideration, this also makes sense. Federal Express is in the overnight delivery business. Obviously, such an endeavor will be affected by the business cycle. When in full swing, business activity is heightened. It becomes important to get that letter to Oshkosh, that bid to Shreveport, that contract to Los Angeles. Companies are willing to spend a little extra to get such correspondence to their destinations overnight.

On the other hand, if the business cycle and business activity are down, cash flows are constricted and office budgets will be cut. Therefore, rather than place the delivery with Federal Express or one of the other overnight delivery services, businesses may be more likely to just stick a stamp on an envelope and trust the U.S. postal system.

PROBLEMS WITH BETAS

It is obvious that betas can be useful in management decision making and investment analysis. However, there are pitfalls and shortcomings associated with using betas in such endeavors.

Past History

Betas are constructed from historical information. They show the relationships between market returns and returns on individual securities in the past. Just because relationships have held true in the past does not mean they will always do so.

A sleepy little drug company may have a beta of .23. If it should suddenly discover a cure for cancer, its returns will shoot up dramatically, regardless of what the market will do.

Likewise, a company in a burgeoning market may have had tremendous growth and a high beta to match. If the market becomes saturated, growth falls, and so does the beta. When the personal computer first started becoming popular, Apple Computer had a beta of over four. Now that the market is more saturated and there is more competition, Apple's beta is less than two.

Instability of Betas

Betas are not necessarily stable. Some companies have shifts in their betas. Some have one beta going up the business cycle and one going down. Some even have random betas, which would obviously be of little use in a practical situation.

At any rate, this possible instability of betas implies that users of betas need to be judicious and do research.

Construction of Betas

Betas may be calculated in different ways. Returns may be calculated on a daily, weekly, monthly, quarterly, or yearly basis. Many different market indicators may be used to calculate market returns. Any number of smoothing techniques may be used in calculating the betas. In other words, several analysts could construct betas for the same stock and come up with different answers. To make matters even more complicated, they might all be technically correct. The time period, market indicator, and technique used to estimate the beta in many cases depend on the use the analyst wants to make of the beta. Again, caution is recommended. Many investment analysts choose to rely on the betas reported in *Value Line Investment Advisory Services,* but the individual situation determines the usefulness of reported betas.

Appendix 3.2: Quantitative Valuation Factors

As stated in Chapter 3, there are any number of techniques for evaluating an individual company's common stocks. In addition to examining qualitative factors, there are numerous quantitative factors to examine. These involve the beta approach, the price/earnings ratios approach, and approaches that look at variations in financial factors, trends in financial factors, and growth in various financial factors. In addition to these factors, many analysts thoroughly examine the company's financial statements. An illustration of financial statement analysis appears in Appendix 3.3.

BETA APPROACHES

Appendix 3.1 discusses betas. If an analyst knows the beta for a company and can calculate the estimated rate of return for the market as a whole, the rate of return for an individual stock may be calculated using the approach described in Chapter 3:

$$r_x = a + b(r_m)$$

where

r_x = rate of return on stock x

a = alpha intercept

b = beta stock x

r_m = return on the market

For example, suppose that, based on past history, the beta for Omega company is known to be 1 and the alpha is 2 percent. Based on leading economic indicators and like data, economic predictions indicate that the rate of return on the market overall is going to be 9 percent. Then the predicted return for Omega is 11% : 2% + 1(9%). If the company is riskier and its beta is 1.2, but the alpha is still 2 percent, then the rate of return would be 12.8% : 2% + 1.2(9%).

A PRICE/EARNINGS RATIOS

The price/earnings ratio is the ratio of the current market price of a stock to the current earnings per share, or,

$$P/E = \frac{MP}{EPS}$$

where

P/E = Price/earnings ratio

MP = Current market price per share

EPS = Current earnings per share

For example, assume a stock currently sells for $30 per share and its current earnings per share are $3. The price/earnings ratio is then 10 − ($30/$3). Price/earnings ratios for many publicly traded stocks are listed in the financial sections of daily newspapers.

Generally, stocks will sell for a multiple of current earnings. The greater the multiple, the greater the market values the future earnings ability of the company.

Some analysts use price/earnings ratios in forecasting stock values. Some figure a normal price/earnings ratio based on past ratios, then predict stock price by multiplying predicted earnings by this normal ratio.

VARIATIONS IN FINANCIAL FACTORS

Many analysts look at past patterns of some financial factors such as stock price, rate of return on stock, and earnings per share. The following discussion of stock price illustrates how it and other financial factors might be analyzed.

Stock Price

Tri-Area Commercial Contractors has the following stock price record:

Year	Price
1981	21
1982	22
1983	22
1984	23

Year	Price
1985	22
1986	24
1987	25
1988	26
1989	27
1990	28

A potential investor might look at the average price of the stock and find it to be $24, the sum of all the stock prices per year, divided by ten years. The range of prices is $21–$28. The standard deviation might also be calculated:

Year	Price	Average	Deviation	Sq. Dev.
1981	21	24	-3	9
1982	22	24	-2	4
1983	22	24	-2	4
1984	23	24	-1	1
1985	22	24	-2	4
1986	24	24	0	0
1987	25	24	1	1
1988	26	24	2	4
1989	27	24	3	9
1990	28	24	4	16

The total of the squared deviations is 52. That divided by 9 $(n-1)$ is 5.78. The square root of 5.78 is 2.4. The standard deviation then is $2.40. Historically, the average of Tri-Area stock is $24. Plus one standard deviation would be $26.40, and minus would be $21.60.

The trend of stock prices, as shown in Figure 3.8, presents a somewhat different picture, however.

Figure 3.8
Stock Price Trend

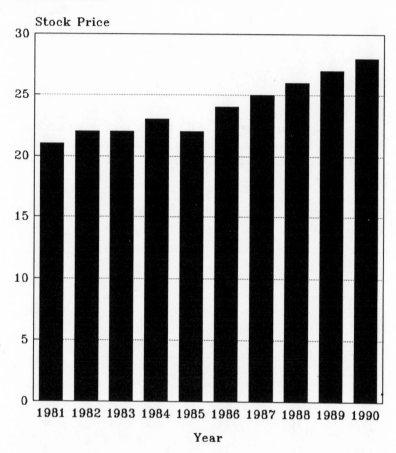

Some analysts study stock price trends and attempt to predict the future of stock price based on past patterns. Known as technical analysis, this is popular with some analysts. Results of research efforts lend little support to notions of technical analysis, however.

Rate of Return on Stock

Stock prices for Tri-Area have already been quoted for the period of 1981–90. Suppose that for those same years dividends per share are:

Year	Div.
1981	$2.00
1982	$2.20
1983	$2.30
1984	$2.40
1985	$2.50
1986	$2.50
1987	$2.60
1988	$2.65
1989	$2.70
1990	$2.75

Assume that the 1980 stock price was $22 per share. Rates of return using the holding period return calculation may then be calculated. For instance, 1981 returns would be calculated by taking the price appreciation between the 1980 stock price and the 1981 stock price ($21–$22). There was a one dollar per share loss in stock price. That same year, however, there was a two dollar per share dividend, so the total return was one dollar. Divided by the base price of $22, this yields a percentage rate of return of about 4.5 percent. Results of rate of return calculations appear below:

Year	Rate
1981	4.5%
1982	15.2%
1983	10.5%
1984	15.5%
1985	6.5%
1986	20.5%
1987	15.0%
1988	14.6%
1989	14.2%
1990	13.9%

The average rate of return is 13 percent. Standard deviation is calculated:

Year	Return	Average	Deviation	Sq. Dev.
1981	4.5	13	-8.5	72.25
1982	15.2	13	2.2	4.84
1983	10.5	13	-2.5	6.25
1984	15.5	13	2.5	6.25
1985	6.5	13	-6.5	42.25
1986	20.5	13	7.5	56.25
1987	15.0	13	2.0	4.00
1988	14.6	13	1.6	2.56
1989	14.2	13	1.2	1.44
1990	13.9	13	.9	.81

The total of squared deviations is 196.9. Variance then is 21.9, so standard deviation is approximately 4.7 percent. The range of outcomes is from 4.5 to 20.5 percent. Plus or minus one standard deviation is 8.3 and 17.7 percent, respectively. A trend appears in Figure 3.9.

Earnings Per Share

The earnings per share for each year are:

Year	EPS
1981	2.10
1982	2.20
1983	2.20
1984	2.30
1985	2.20
1986	2.40
1987	2.50
1988	2.60
1989	2.70
1990	2.80

Figure 3.9
Rate of Returns Trend

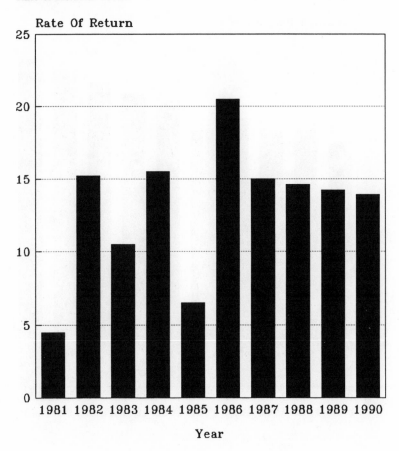

Rate Of Return

Average earnings per share then are $2.40 with a standard deviation of just .10. In this case it is interesting to note that for every year Tri-Area stock price was 10 times earnings per share. In other words, Tri-Area had a very stable price/earnings ratio of 10. The trend is shown in Figure 3.10.

Figure 3.10
Earnings per Share Trend

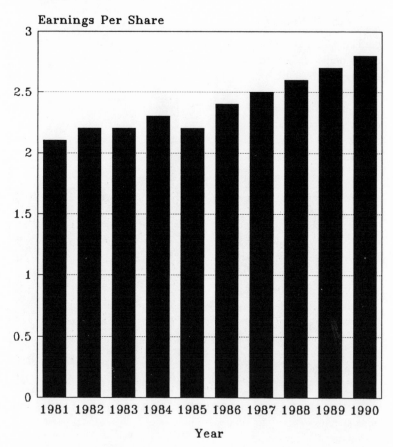

An analyst would probably never rely completely on financial factors. However, when examined in conjunction with other factors already outlined and a good financial statement analysis, a complete security valuation may be achieved.

Appendix 3.3: Financial Statement Analysis

In analyzing potential corporate stock investments, financial statements are valuable sources of information. They are not necessarily perfect; accounting rules and practices are nowhere near uniform between preparers. Quirks and foibles abound; however, in the absence of other usable information, financial statements must be necessarily exploited for clues as to the potential of the underlying company.

To understand how the statements may be used for chasing down clues, it is necessary to first understand how statements are put together, how information is presented on the statements, what that information indicates, and how it may be manipulated for further detail.

BASIC FINANCIAL STATEMENTS

Statements basic to most companies are the balance sheet, the income statement, and the statement of changes in financial position. Each of these statements is put together differently, and each contains different types of information. The following section examines each type of statement and itemizes characteristics of the balance sheet and the income statement as well as what sort of information is included in each. Because of the special nature of the statement of changes in financial position, it is covered separately in Appendix 3.4.

The Balance Sheet

The balance sheet is a listing of the firm's assets and the claims against those assets, as of a particular date. The balance sheet thus shows what a firm owes and what it owns. There are a number of points that might be made about the balance sheet.

1. The balance sheet has to balance: the assets must equal the total claims against the company on that date.
2. Items on the balance sheet are listed in order of liquidity. For assets, liquidity means "nearness to cash." So cash and near-cash items are listed first. Longer-term assets, those not easily converted to cash, will be listed toward the bottom of the assets side. For claims, liquidity refers to how quickly the claim against the company will mature.

3. Assets are valued at original cost. Exceptions are marketable securities and inventories. These are valued at lower of cost or market.

A sample balance sheet appears in Table 3.4. An explanation of the various balance sheet items follows.

Cash: Includes cash on hand and in banks.

Marketable securities: Short-term investments of the company in bonds, stocks, government securities, etc.

Accounts receivable: Monies owed by customers on account.

Inventories: Include raw materials, work-in-process, and finished goods inventories.

Plant and equipment: Long-term assets owned by the company, valued at cost. If the company owns the land on which a plant sits, that should be listed separately, because land does not depreciate.

Accumulated depreciation: A "contra-asset" account. This shows total depreciation accrued against the asset. Plant and equipment, less the depreciation account, equal the net balance.

Other long-term assets: Might include good will or the like.

Accounts payable: Total owed on open account to others.

Notes payable: Short-term notes borrowed.

Accruals: Services received but not yet paid for. An example might be accrued taxes.

Bonds: Long-term borrowings. (Not shown in Table 3.4.)

Preferred stock: Equity instrument that has preference over common stock. (Not shown in Table 3.4.)

Common stock: Total of this account is the number of shares of common stock outstanding times the par value of the stock.

Surplus: Sometimes called paid-in capital in excess of par. This account shows residual of proceeds from stock offerings less the common stock account. For instance, assume a company sold 100,000 shares of common stock at $5 per share, but the par value of the stock was only $1 per share. Then $100,000 would be recorded for the common stock account (100,000 × $1) and $400,000 for the paid-in surplus account (100,000 [$5 − $1]).

Retained earnings: This represents all accumulated profits of the company since its inception. It is also the total of all transfers to retained earnings off all income statements since the company's inception.

Table 3.4
Sample Balance Sheet

ASSETS

Cash	$ 47,500
Marketable Securities	15,000
Accounts Receivable	112,000
Inventories	190,000

Total Current	364,500

Plant and Equipment	590,000
Accumulated Depreciation	(290,000)
Net Fixed Assets	300,000
Other Long-term Assets	10,000

Total Long-Term Assets	310,000

TOTAL ASSETS	674,500

CLAIMS ON ASSETS

Accounts Payable	$ 32,000
Notes Payable	50,000
Accruals	5,000
Total Current	87,000
Long-Term Liabilities	174,500

Total Liabilities	261,500

Common Stock & Surplus	400,000
Retained Earnings	13,000
Total Owners' Equity	413,000

TOTAL CLAIMS ON ASSETS	674,500

Income Statement

The income statement shows a firm's revenues and the costs, expenses, and taxes associated with those revenues for some financial period, such as a month, quarter, or year. Table 3.5 shows a sample income statement. A brief explanation of these items follows.

Sales: Shows total revenue from sales less returns and allowances for the financial period. If there are revenues from nonoperating or extraordinary sources, they would not be included here.

Cost of goods sold: The costs of producing or selling the company's product, including materials, labor, and overhead.

Gross profit: Sales less cost of goods sold.

Selling and administrative expenses: Expenses from other than operations.

Leases: Self-explanatory.

Earnings before interest and taxes: Sales minus all expenses to this point in statement.

Interest: Costs of borrowings.

Table 3.5
Income Statement

Total Sales	$1,350,000
Less: Cost of Goods Sold	800,000
Gross Operating Profits	550,000
Less: Selling and Administrative Expenses	200,000
Less: Leases	100,000
Earnings Before Interest and Taxes	250,000
Less: Interest Expenses	50,000
Taxable Earnings	200,000
Less: Taxes	100,000
Net Income	100,000
Less: Dividends	10,000
Transfer to Retained Earnings	90,000

Earnings before taxes: Sales minus all expenses to this point in statement.

Taxes: Taxes due on revenues less expenses.

Earnings after taxes: Sometimes called net income. The amount available to owners of the company. Owners can divide profits through dividends, plow profits back into the company, or combine the two.

Dividends: Profits disseminated to owners.

Transfer to retained earnings: Net income minus dividends.

RATIO ANALYSIS

Based on the information contained in financial statements, ratios may be calculated. For a full understanding of ratio analysis, explanations of the groups and calculation of ratios and an interpretation of ratios are included. A sample based on the balance sheet (Table 3.4) and income statement (Table 3.5) included in this appendix is also included.

Classification of Ratios

There are any number of ways to classify ratios, but four general classifications are recognized by most financial analysts. These are liquidity ratios, turnover ratios, profitability ratios, and debt ratios. Table 3.6 shows classifications of ratios, major ratios in each category, how to calculate individual ratios, and gives an explanation of each of these major ratios.

Liquidity Ratios

Liquidity ratios reflect the current position of the company. They illustrate how well prepared the company is to meet maturing short-term obligations. Two major liquidity ratios are the current ratio and the quick ratio. The current ratio is calculated by dividing current assets by current liabilities. Current assets are cash, marketable securities, accounts receivable, and inventories. Chief current liabilities are accounts payable, notes payable, and accruals. The current ratio, then, indicates how many times current assets will cover current liabilities. In an unstable environment, one where it is difficult to predict cash inflows and outflows, it might be desirable to have a higher current ratio then another company better able to predict its cash flows.

Table 3.6
Ratios

LIQUIDITY -   Measure the firm's ability to meet maturing
               short-term obligations.

          RATIO   CALCULATION

                                         Current Assets
          Current   Current Liabilities

               Shows how many times current assets
               cover current liabilities.

                                         Quick Assets
          Quick   Current Liabilities

               Shows how may times "quick assets" cover
               current liabilities.

TURNOVER -   Show a firm's ability to utilize
              resources to generate sales.

                                    Sales
          Total Asset Turnover   Total Assets

               Shows how a company uses all the assets
               at its disposal to generate sales.

                                    Sales
          Fixed Asset Turnover   Fixed Assets

               Shows how a firm uses fixed assets to
               generate sales.

                                Sales
          Inventory Turnover   Inventories

               Shows how a firm uses inventories in
               generating sales.

Table 3.6 (Continued)

PROFITABILITY -Show efficiency with which management
operates.

Net Profit Margin	$\dfrac{\text{Net Income After Taxes}}{\text{Total Sales}}$

Shows percent net income is of total sales.

Gross Profit Margin	$\dfrac{\text{Gross Operating Profits}}{\text{Total Sales}}$

Shows profitability of operations.

Return on Equity	$\dfrac{\text{Net Income After Taxes}}{\text{Owners' Equity}}$

Shows returns to shareholders.

Return on Assets	$\dfrac{\text{Net Income After Taxes}}{\text{Total Assets}}$

Illustrates profitability compared to total
asset base.

DEBT RATIO   Illustrate extent to which the firm is
financed by debt.

Debt Ratio	$\dfrac{\text{Total Liabilities}}{\text{Total Assets}}$

Show percent of total capital financed by
debt.

Table 3.6 (Continued)

	Earnings Before Interest & Taxes
Times Interest Earned	Interest Charges

Shows how many times earnings will cover
fixed interest payments.

	Income Available
Fixed Charge Coverage	for Fixed Charges
	Fixed Charges*

Shows how many times earnings will cover
fixed charges.

*Fixed Charges are calculated by summing earnings before
interest and taxes, lease payments and preferred dividend
payments.

The quick ratio is another liquidity ratio. It is calculated by dividing quick assets by current liabilities. Quick assets are cash, marketable securities, and accounts receivable. Therefore, the quick ratio omits the influence of inventories, which are not so easily converted to cash as the other current assets.

Turnover ratios

Turnover ratios illustrate the firm's ability to utilize resources at its disposal in generating sales. These ratios do not show the efficiency used in generating sales, but rather the raw ability of a company to generate sales. Chief turnover ratios are the total asset turnover ratio, the fixed asset turnover ratio, and the inventory turnover ratio.

The total asset turnover ratio shows how a company uses all the assets at its disposal in generating sales. It is calculated by dividing total sales or revenues (after returns and allowances) by total assets of the firm.

Fixed asset turnover is calculated by dividing total sales by net fixed assets of the company. Fixed asset turnover shows how many times greater sales are than net fixed assets.

Inventory turnover is calculated by dividing total sales by inventories. It is best to use an average inventory (over a year or several months) if information is available.

Profitability ratios

These ratios show a firm's efficiency. Chief among profitability ratios are net profit margin, gross profit margin, return on equity, and return on assets. The net profit margin is calculated by dividing net earnings after taxes by total sales. The gross profit margin results when gross profits are divided by sales. Return on equity is found by dividing earnings after taxes by shareholders' equity. The return on assets is earnings after taxes divided by total assets.

Debt ratios

These ratios show the extent to which the firm is financed by debt, and the impact of that debt on the company. Chief debt ratios are the debt ratio, the times interest earned ratio (TIE), and the fixed charge coverage ratio (FCC).

The debt ratio shows the extent to which the firm is financed by debt. It is calculated by dividing total liabilities or debt by total assets. In judging whether or not a level of debt is or is not too high, it is helpful to look at how many times the firm can cover fixed debt payments with the income it generates. Two ratios that reflect this are the TIE ratio and the FCC ratio. The TIE ratio is calculated by dividing earnings before interest and taxes by fixed interest payments. The FCC ratio is calculated by dividing income available for meeting fixed charges by total fixed charges. Fixed charges include interest payments, fixed lease obligations, and preferred dividend payments. The income available for meeting fixed charges, then, would be earnings before interest and taxes plus fixed lease payments and preferred dividend payments. An example of these ratios that have been calculated for the financial statements included in this appendix appear in Table 3.7.

Table 3.7
Sample Ratios

RATIO	CALCULATION	RESULT
Current	$\dfrac{364,500}{87,000}$	4.19
Quick	$\dfrac{364,500 - 190,000}{87,000}$	2.00
Total Asset Turnover	$\dfrac{1,350,000}{674,500}$	2.00
Fixed Asset Turnover	$\dfrac{1,350,000}{310,000}$	4.35
Inventory Turnover	$\dfrac{1,350,000}{190,000}$	7.10
Net Profit Margin	$\dfrac{100,000}{1,350,000}$	0.07
Gross Profit Margin	$\dfrac{550,000}{1,350,000}$	0.41
Return on Assets	$\dfrac{100,000}{674,500}$	0.15
Debt Ratio	$\dfrac{261,500}{674,500}$	0.39
Times Interest Earned	$\dfrac{250,000}{50,000}$	5.00
Fixed Charges Coverage	$\dfrac{350,000}{150,000}$	2.33

Appendix 3.4: Statement of Changes in Financial Position

The statement of changes in financial position can be a good clue to potential investors as to the quality of a company's management. The statement shows an important facet of management—namely, how well a firm manages the flow of funds through its operations.

FUNDS FLOW

All financial management of a firm revolves around two functions: financing and investing. The financing function raises capital and brings it into the company. The investing function puts that capital to work. An inherent principle of management should be to put raised funds to work in ways that will generate returns greater than the costs to raise them. A good firm will of course put every dollar to work in the one use that will optimize returns. An analysis of the funds flow aids potential investors in gauging how well a firm performs this important function.

EXAMPLE OF FUNDS ANALYSIS

Assume a potential investor is interested in two different companies—Company A and Company B. The investor obtains financial statements for each company, then decides to look at the balance sheet to get a feel for the financial health of each company. The investor next examines the most important item on the balance sheet—total assets. The results appear thus:

	Company A	Company B
total assets	$123,785 million	$14,000 million

Which of the companies is better? It is impossible to tell based on this information alone. A is clearly bigger than B, but bigger is not necessarily better.

Next, the investor examines the most important piece of information on the income statement—net income. The results are:

	Company A	Company B
net income	$14,890 million	$1.230 million

Again, it is impossible to identify the best company.

Now, suppose the investor examines the chief sources and the chief uses of funds for each company. The results are summarized:

	Company A	Company B
sources	borrowed funds	retained earnings
uses	paid-off old debt	bought new plant and equipment

Now B looks more promising than A. B appears to be investing in the future. Its chief use of funds appears to be an investment in productive facilities. The source of financing for such growth is the company's retained earnings—profits that have been plowed back into the firm.

A looks like it is borrowing from Peter to pay Paul. It is a company that has grown quite large in the past, but is now perhaps in the maturity phase of its growth cycle. That is not to say that A is doing anything wrong. It may be they feel this strategy is optimal. Perhaps the old debt was financed at 18 percent and the new debt can be financed at 10 percent. This refinancing move, then, may be the best use of funds they could undertake at this time. More analysis is certainly called for.

No investor should, of course, make investment decisions on such sketchy information. This only illustrates the kinds of insights that may be gleaned from examining the sources and uses of funds.

DETERMINATION OF SOURCES AND USES OF FUNDS

There are several steps involved in determining the sources and uses of funds.

1. Compare a beginning and ending balance sheet;
2. identify the changes as to whether they are sources or uses of funds;
3. prepare the statement according to the desired format.

Consider a company with the statements as illustrated in Table 3.8. Changes in balance sheet items would appear as in Table 3.9.

To classify these changes as to whether they are sources or uses of funds, picture the flow of funds. Anything that increases the pool of

Table 3.8
Balance Sheets

	Beginning of Year	End of Year
Cash	$30*	$14
Securities	22	0
Receivables	44	60
Inventories	55	75
Net Fixed Assets	50	150
Total Assets	201	299
Payables	30	36
Other Current	30	10
Long-Term Debt	50	110
Common Stock	75	100
Retained Earnings	16	43
Total Claims	201	299

*In Millions of Dollars

funds available to the firm would be a source of funds. Anything that would be drawn out of the pool of funds is a use of funds. A simple decision rule exists: a source of funds is (1) an increase in a liability item and (2) a decrease in an asset item; a use of funds is (1) an increase in an asset item and (2) a decrease in a liability item. The classification of sources and uses for the firm in question appears in Table 3.10.

Table 3.9
Changes in Balance Sheet Items

	Beg. of Yr.	End of Yr.	Change
Cash	$30	$14	-16
Securities	22	0	-22
Receivables	44	60	+16
Inventories	55	75	+20
Net Fixed Assets	50	150	+100
Payables	30	36	+6
Other Current	30	10	-20
Long-Term Debt	50	110	+60
Common Stock	75	100	+25
Retained Earnings	16	43	+27

Table 3.10
Sources and Uses of Funds

Item	Source	Use
Cash	16	
Securities	22	
Receivables		16
Inventories		20
Net Fixed Assets		100
Payables	6	
Other Current		20
Long-Term Debt	60	
Common Stock	25	
Retained Earnings	27	
TOTAL	156	156

Table 3.11
Funds Statement

Sources of Funds:

Increase in Long-Term Debt	$60*
Increase in Retained Earnings	27
Increase in Common Stock	25
Decrease in Marketable Securities	22
Decrease in Cash	16
Increase in Accounts Payable	6
TOTAL SOURCES OF FUNDS	156

Uses of Funds:

Increase in Fixed Assets	100
Increase in Inventories	20
Decrease in Current Liabilities	20
Increase in Accounts Receivable	16
TOTAL USES:	156

*In Millions of Dollars

The next step is to prepare the statement. Accountants formally present statements of changes in financial position when part of an annual report. The statement may be prepared on a working capital basis, which lumps a great deal of information together, or on a cash basis, which looks at each balance sheet item change separately. Presently, but subject to change, most firms prepare their statements on a working capital basis. Consequently, the formal statement included in an annual report may not always be as good a source of information to a potential investor as a "homemade" version as illustrated in Table 3.11.

An analysis of this statement leads the observer to have serious doubts about the future of this company. Its current liabilities are building up, net profits are negative, and at the same time the company's asset base is shrinking. The potential for trouble is apparent.

The statement of changes in financial position, or, more accurately, a homemade version of the statement, can be a useful tool to potential investors. It should, however, be used in conjunction with other tools outlined in this chapter.

4

Sources of Financial Information

As mentioned, information links corporate events and stock prices. Information in today's world is immediate. Information affects the way people work and play, and also the way they make money.

In the United States it is easy to trace technological influences historically and see the resultant effect on economic institutions.

During the nation's early history, financial activity in the United States was relatively unhurried. Agriculture was the primary economic activity, and financial transactions revolved around farming and related activities. There was usually a direct relationship between the provider and the user of funds.

With the coming of the industrial revolution, many diverse industries were established. With this economic growth came the need for funds, and financial transactions were necessarily made more rapidly than before. This prompted the establishment of different kinds of financial institutions, leading to increased activity in financial markets. The keys to financial activity during this period were speed and variety. No longer was there a direct relationship between the providers and users of funds.

The author wishes to thank Geri Hutchins for assisting in compiling this chapter.

Perhaps the industrial age is past, and the information revolution has already taken place. Because of rapid advances in technology, information is transmitted nearly instantaneously, leading to the transition from a manufacturing to a service economy. It also means that financial activity has shifted into another dimension—rapid-fire transactions. Fortunes change hands every second. To survive in this environment, a trader needs information and the ability to apply it.

As mentioned previously, an abundance of information is available to assist investors. The following sources of information will help in formulating earnings estimates, such as the processes outlined in Chapter 3.

There are countless sources of financial information available to potential investors or anyone who wants information about financial resources. Indeed, the volume of information may overwhelm the researcher. The listing of sources here is by no means inclusive, but merely a guide to major resources. The listing has been divided into several categories to make it more accessible.

GUIDES TO THE LITERATURE AND DIRECTORIES

There are a number of different guides to financial literature. One of the better known is *Business Information Sources* by Lorna Daniells (Berkeley, Calif.: University of California Press, 1985), an excellent tool for determining relevant sources of business information. All entries are annotated and arranged in subject order.

Many directories are available to assist in quick reference checks, or to begin a more extensive search of financial information. The directories below are listed in order of importance.

Unless specified, all are updated annually.

Dun's Million Dollar Directory (Parsippany, N.J.: Dun's Marketing Services) is extensive (five volumes) and lists over 115,000 companies with an indicated worth of over $500,000. Each entry includes names of officers and directors; principal lines of business; SIC codes; company sales; number of employees; ticker symbol; and principal bank, law firm, and accounting firm. Information is arranged alphabetically by corporate name. Separate volumes contain indexes by SIC code and geographic location.

Dun's Business Rankings (Parsippany, N.J.: Dun's Marketing Services) ranks public and private companies according to sales and employee size.

Reference Book of Corporate Management (Parsippany, N.J.: Dun's Marketing Services) is four volumes of leading U.S. companies, and includes top executives' birth dates, college degrees, marital status, and past positions. The names and titles of other officers are also included.

Principal International Businesses (New York: Dun and Bradstreet) lists leading companies in 133 countries, arranged alphabetically. Information includes chief officer, line of business, telex and SIC numbers, approximate sales and number of employees, and export/import and subsidiary status.

Standard and Poor's Register of Corporations (New York: Standard and Poor's) is contained in three volumes. Volume 1 contains an alphabetical list of over 40,000 companies; including such information as names of officers; line of business; SIC codes; sales; number of employees; accounting firm, major bank and law firm; and stock exchange symbol. Some large subsidiaries are listed apart from their parent companies. Volume 2 is a directory of executives and directors, with brief biographical entries. Volume 3 contains several indexes and lists, including a list of companies by SIC codes and geographical location, corporate family indexes, and other related indexes.

Thomas Register of American Manufacturers and *Thomas Register Catalog* (New York: Thomas Publishing) is a 21-volume annual directory of American manufacturing firms. Products and services are listed in Volumes 1–12. Volumes 13–14 contain company profiles arranged alphabetically by company name, addresses, branch offices, subsidiaries, products, and asset classification. Volumes 15–21 describe supplier's catalogs, brochures, and related literature.

Ward's Major U.S. Private Companies (Belmont, Calif.: Information Access) is a directory of private companies with sales in excess of $500,000. Companies can be accessed in three ways: by sales within SIC codes, by zip code under state, and alphabetically. Information includes addresses, sales, chief executive officer (CEO), phone numbers, SIC codes, number of employees, and year founded.

Directory of Corporate Affiliations (Wilmette, Ill.: National Register Publishing) is useful in determining parent companies, affiliates and subsidiaries. An index in the front of the volumes gives access to both parent companies and their subsidiaries. Each entry includes the address of the parent company, officers, telephone numbers, sales, number of employees, and SIC codes. Similar entries for affiliates and subsidiaries are included.

America's Corporate Families (Parsippany, N.J.: Dun's Marketing Services) is a directory of approximately 9,200 corporate families and their affiliates. Criteria for selection includes two or more corporate locations, and net worth of over $500,000 and controlling interest in one or more subsidiary. Indexed alphabetically, geographically, and by SIC code. Contains addresses, officers, and other information.

Rand McNally International Bankers Directory, 4 vols. (Chicago, Ill.: Rand McNally, 1983). Volumes 1–2 is a U.S. master alphabetical list of banks by state and city and includes addresses, financial information, officers, and branches, among other information. Volume 3 is U.S. operating information for check processing and fund transfers for chartered banks. Volume 4 contains information about international banks.

Directory of American Savings and Loan Associations (Baltimore: T. K. Sanderson) is a geographic list of U.S. savings and loan associations, and provides officers, branches, total assets, and interest rate, among other information.

Directory of Industry Data Sources (Belmont, Calif.: Information Access Company) is three volumes of industry-intensive data covering the United States and Canada. For each major four-digit SIC industry code, the following information is included: market research reports, industry statistical reports, financial and economic studies, investment banking reports, conference reports, and indexes and abstracts.

The World Directory of Multinational Enterprise (Detroit: Gale Research).

Directory of Foreign Manufacturers in the United States (Atlanta: Georgia State University, Business Publishing Division).

Marconi's International Register, Telegraphic Cable and Radio Registrations (Mamaroneck, N.Y.) lists postal addresses and telex or telephone numbers of the world's principal firms having international contact.

INDEXES TO PERIODICAL AND NEWSPAPER ARTICLES

A number of different indexes guide the user in finding information about different financial topics in newspapers and business periodicals:

- *ABA (American Bankers Association) Banking Literature Index* (Washington, D.C.: American Bankers Association).
- *Index of Economic Articles* (Homewood, Ill.: R. D. Irwin).
- *Business Periodicals Index* (New York: H. W. Wilson).
- *Predicasts' F and S Index* (Cleveland: Predicasts) is indexed by SIC code and company name and includes many trade journals.
- *Accountant's Index* (New York: American Institute of Certified Public Accountants).
- *The National Newspaper Index* includes indexing for *Wall Street Journal, Barron's, New York Times, Washington Post, Christian Science Monitor,* and *Los Angeles Times.* Published by Information Access Company, Mountainview, California.
- *The Wall Street Journal Index* (Princeton: Dow Jones) indexes *Wall Street Journal* articles, grouped by corporate and general news.

STATISTICAL SOURCES

Data on countless topics may be found in a number of statistical services.

Standard and Poor's Statistical Service (New York: Standard and Poor's) arranges current and basic statistics in the following areas: banking and finance; production and labor; price indexes (commodities, producer indexes, and cost of living); income and trade; building; electric power and fuels; metals; transportation; textiles, chemicals and paper; agricultural products; and security price index record (Standard and Poor's stock price indexes, Dow Jones averages).

Predicasts Forecasts (Cleveland: Predicasts) includes short- and long-range forecasts for leading economic indicators, statistics on specific U.S. industries and products, and bibliographic information on current journals from which the data is taken.

U.S. Industrial Outlook, compiled by U.S. Bureau of Economic Analysis (Washington, D.C.: U.S. Department of Commerce), includes trends and outlook for 250 U.S. manufacturing and nonmanufacturing industries.

Survey of Current Business (Washington, D.C.: G.P.O.), a complete and reliable source for current U.S. business statistics, includes general business indicators, commodity prices, construction and real estate, domestic trade, and foreign trade, among other information. Special statistical reports also appear such as the annual National Income and Products Accounts issue. Also prepared by the U.S. Bureau of Economic Analysis, Department of Commerce.

Business Conditions Digest, prepared and published by U.S. Department of Commerce, contains charts and statistics for leading economic times series. Arranged in two parts: cyclical indicators (150 time series) and other important economic measures (140 series covering national income and products, among other things).

Federal Reserve Bulletin (Washington, D.C.: G.P.O.) is a monthly periodical that is one of the best sources for current U.S. banking and monetary statistics. Includes data such as interest rates on money markets, stock market indexes, consumer credit, and interest and exchange rates. The board also publishes a Federal Reserve Chart Book, which includes the most important statistics from the bulletin.

Industry Norms and Key Business Ratios, compiled by Dun and Bradstreet (Parsippany, N.J.: Dun and Bradstreet), this publication is an annual compilation of 14 key business ratios and related statistical information about industries. Arranged by SIC code, the ratio data is compiled from balance sheets and other relevant financial documents. These key business ratios cover "critical areas of business performance with indicators of solvency, efficiency, and profitability. Ratios are broken down into median figures with upper and lower quartiles.

RMA Annual Statement Studies (Philadelphia: Robert Morris and Ass.) is arranged by SIC codes. Financial data is similar to Dun and Bradstreet's Industry Norms, but is presented somewhat differently. Assets, liabilities, and income data for industries are included.

Monthly Labor Review (Washington, D.C.: U.S. Bureau of Labor Statistics) provides information on employment, unemployment, hours, earnings, consumer and wholesale prices, productivity, and labor management data.

SEC Monthly Statistics Review (Washington, D.C.: U.S. Securities and Exchange Commission) gives statistical data on new securities offerings, registrations, and volume and value of trading on exchanges.

Also included are quarterly or semiannual statistics on working capital (current assets and liabilities of nonfinancial organizations), assets of noninsured pension funds, and foreign securities sold in the United States.

Economic Indicators (Washington, D.C.: G.P.O.).

Producer Price Indexes (Washington, D.C.: U.S. Department of Labor and Bureau of Labor Statistics).

CPI Detailed Report (Washington, D.C.: U.S. Department of Labor and Bureau of Labor Statistics).

Employment and Earnings (Washington, D.C.: U.S. Department of Labor and Bureau of Labor Statistics).

Census of Manufacturers (Washington, D.C.: U.S. Bureau of the Census) reports information on 450 manufacturing industries in every state, including number of establishments, value of shipments, cost of materials, capital expenditures, assets, rents, inventories, employment and payrolls. An annual survey of manufacturers is published in the years between each census, giving statistics for broad industry groups and selected products.

Census of Government (Washington, D.C.: U.S. Bureau of the Census) details statistics on government finance.

Census of Retail Trade (Washington, D.C.: U.S. Bureau of the Census) gives statistics for approximately one hundred different kinds of retail enterprises by state, SMSA, and areas outside SMSA's, including number of establishments, sales, payroll, and employment. A special report on size provides data based on sales and employment size and legal form of organization.

Census of Wholesale Trade (Washington, D.C.: U.S. Bureau of the Census) gives data for wholesale businesses, including number of establishments, sales, payroll, employment, operating expenses, size, legal form of organization, type of operation, and a special report on wholesale commodity line sales.

Statistical Abstract of the United States (Washington, D.C.: U.S. Department of Commerce).

GENERAL CORPORATE INFORMATION

Moody's Manuals (New York: Moody's Investor Source) are comprised of eight separate financial manuals: *Moody's Bank and Finance*

Manual, Moody's Industrial Manual, Moody's International Manual, Moody's Municipal and Government Manual, Moody's OTC Industrial Manual, Moody's OTC Unlisted Manual, Moody's Public Utilities Manual, Moody's Transportation Manual, and *Moody's Complete Corporate Index* (three per year). Annual volumes include monthly news reports.

With the exception of *Moody's International Manual,* these volumes contain companies listed on the exchanges or traded "over the counter." There are two possible types of coverage for each company. Complete coverage includes information such as capital structure, corporate history, subsidiaries, properties, officers, CEO's letter to stockholders, seven-year income and balance sheet statistics, number of stockholders, number of employees, and other data from the annual report. The other type of coverage, full measure or comprehensive coverage, contains less information. Moody's averages, Moody's Commodity Price Index (monthly since 1933), a list of industrial stock splits, stock purchase warrants, and other information are included. An index of companies by industry and location is also included. *Moody's Complete Corporate Index* is useful for determining the appropriate manual.

Standard and Poor's Corporation Records (New York: Standard and Poor's) is a six-volume set arranged in loose-leaf format with bimonthly supplements. Comparable to Moody's, covering companies with listed and unlisted securities (*Daily News* section). Arranged alphabetically and by company size. An index to companies and subsidiaries is in the front of each volume.

FINANCIAL SERVICES

A host of financial services is available, although most can be quite costly. Major libraries in universities and municipalities have most relevant sources, however.

Value Line Investment Survey (New York: A. Bernhard) is in a loose-leaf format with weekly supplements. Reports and analyzes data on 1,700 public companies in about 95 industries. Provides statistics, charts, and explanatory text for each company and industry. Data is reviewed and updated on a rotating basis so that data is updated quarterly. The information given for each company includes: 11-year statistical history of 22 investment factors, plus three 5-year forecasts, quarterly sales, EPS, dividends, Value Line ratings (on timeliness, safety, and Beta), a review of current developments, and future estimates.

Value Line has three parts: Part 1 is summary and index and Part 3 is ratings and reports. Part 2, selection and options filed separately, contains information on business and financial outlooks, investment advice, data on one "especially recommended" stock, and Value Line stock price averages.

Wiesenberger Investment Companies Service and supplements (New York: Wiesenberger Financial Services) provides information on investment companies and mutual funds. Also includes topics such as how to chart an investment course, choosing an investment company, and how to appraise management records.

Each of four parts focuses on a particular aspect of investment. Part 1 contains general information, and Part 2 lists investment companies and a glossary of investment terms. Part 3 covers mutual funds, money market funds, tax-exempt municipal funds, unit trusts, and a table of mutual funds registered in the United States. Part 4 covers closed-end investment companies, mutual fund investment companies, and the "Wiesenberger Mutual Fund Indexes." Supplements include Current Performance and Dividend Record (monthly) and Management Results (quarterly). Both provide current statistics.

The Outlook (New York: Standard and Poor's) is a monthly advisory service on prospects in the stock market. Analyzes trends and includes some information on individual securities, provides purchase recommendations, and lists Standard and Poor's stock market indexes.

Credit Week (New York: Standard and Poor's) is a weekly service that looks at the trends and prospects for money market funds, corporate and government bonds, and other fixed income funds. Each issue includes a list of recent offerings by sales date, ratings, and Standard and Poor's market indexes.

Mutual Fund Yearbook (Homewood, Ill.: Dow Jones-Irwin) is a guide for individuals wanting to invest in no-load mutual funds.

Johnson's Charts (Buffalo, N.Y.: Johnson's Charts, Inc.) provides an analysis of the corporative characteristics and investment performance of mutual funds.

STOCKS AND BONDS

Information on individual stocks and bonds is readily available to most investors. Again, most of these sources are quite expensive, although many are available in larger libraries.

Moody's Bond Survey (New York: Moody's Investors Service) is updated weekly and focuses on trends and outlooks for the market and for individual bonds with purchase or sales recommendations. The survey updates ratings and other information and includes Moody's yield averages, a Moody's financing calendar, and ratings of preferred stock.

Moody's Bond Record: Corporates, Convertibles, Governments, Municipals, and Commercial Paper Ratings, Preferred Stock Ratings (New York: Moody's Investors Service) is a monthly source with information on over 32,000 bonds. It includes prices, interest rates, price range, maturity yields, ratings, issue dates, and amounts outstanding.

Standard and Poor's Bond Guide (New York: Standard and Poor's) includes financial tables on American and a few foreign bonds, including convertibles. It also includes Standard and Poor's ratings on corporate and municipal bonds.

Moody's Dividend Record (New York: Moody's Investors Service) and *Standard and Poor's Dividend Record* (New York: Standard and Poor's) both cover declarations and payments of cash and stock dividends, stock splits, stockholder's rights issued, and tax status of dividends.

Standard and Poor's Stock Reports (New York: Standard and Poor's) gives business summaries, developments, income, balance sheet and per share data, capitalization, dividends, and other relevant information. This source is divided into three separate sets with four volumes in each set. *Standard ASE Stock Reports, Standard NYSE Stock Reports, Standard OTC Stock Reports,* and a supplement, *OTC Profiles.*

Standard and Poor's Daily Stock Price Record (New York: Standard and Poor's) includes three services, one for each market (American Stock Exchange, New York Stock Exchange, and over-the-counter market). Provides daily and weekly records of the volume, high/low, and closing price for each stock. Also includes, at the front of each volume, daily market indicators, such as Dow Jones averages.

Unlisted Market Guide (Glen Head, N.Y.: The Unlisted Market Service Corporation) contains similar information to Standard and Poor's, but also includes data on obscure or small over-the-counter companies.

Moody's Handbook of Common Stocks (New York: Moody's Investors Service) is a quarterly that contains basic financial information on over nine hundred high-interest stocks. The handbook contains price charts and financial data (capitalization, quarterly earnings, dividends, EPS, P/E ratios, and institutional holdings), some covering a ten-year period, for each stock.

GENERAL INDUSTRY INFORMATION

A number of sources contain broad industry information:

Standard and Poor's Industry Surveys (New York: Standard and Poor's) contains data for 33 industries, and is updated quarterly and annually. It includes financial comparisons of the leading companies in each industry.

Quarterly Financial Report for Manufacturing, Mining, and Trade Corporations, prepared by the Federal Trade Commission (Washington, D.C.: G.P.O.), includes a quarterly income statement and balance sheet for 22 manufacturing industries, as well as other selected financial information.

FINANCIAL NEWSPAPERS AND MAGAZINES

Several financial newspapers and magazines focus on topics of interest to the financial community, including general news stories, financial quotes, and in-depth analyses of financial trends:

Fortune (New York)

Business Week (New York: McGraw-Hill)

Barron's (New York: Dow Jones)

Forbes (New York)

Wall Street Journal (New York: Dow Jones)

5

How to Measure Impact of Corporate Events on Firm Stock Price

To understand the impact of corporate events on common stock prices and issues pertinent to event methodology, it might be helpful to discuss an example.

Take a relatively simple corporate event, such as an announcement of a common stock offering. It is not an earth-shaking move, there is no tragedy, no grand opera to be played out before the media—just an ordinary corporate event. It is an event that might have an impact on the stock price of a firm, however.

For instance, on September 26, 1989, such companies as Energy Service, Mass Microsystems, Lattice Semiconductor, Marietta, and even Mustang Ranch offered common stock for sale. Some of the stocks of these companies went up after the announcement. Just because the stock went up, however, doesn't mean that the announcement caused the jump. The stock market could have been booming. In fact, if the rest of the market gained 30 percent the day after the announcement, and one of the companies' stock only gained 5 percent, then maybe the announcement actually hurt the company.

It is then necessary to figure out the price the company's stock would have sold for without the stock sale announcement and compare that to the actual price. Any difference might then be attributable to the announcement of the stock sale. Subtract the price stock *should* have sold for if event had not occurred from the *actual* price, and the result is the price attributable to stock offering.

How can someone predict the stock price without the stock offering? Recall valuation concepts from Chapter 3, which discussed risk and return. At the end of the chapter the notion that individual stock prices might be related to market returns was introduced, as well as a model for estimating returns on individual stocks. Simply stated, that model was:

$$r_x = a + b(r_m) + e$$

where

r_x = rate of return on an individual stock x

a = alpha intercept

b = slope of line

r_m = rate of return on the market

e = error coefficient

The *y* intercept, *a* in the equation, is commonly referred to as alpha. The *b* in the equation is sometimes called the beta of the stock. (An appendix to Chapter 3 briefly explores the notion of beta.) Frequently, the error coefficient is neglected in practical usage.

Therefore, if the computed alpha of a stock is 3 percent, the beta is 2 and the predicted rate of return on the market is to be 10 percent, then the predicted rate of return on that stock would be 23 percent.

$$\begin{aligned} r_x &= a + b_{(m)} \\ &= 3 + 2(10) \\ &= 23 \end{aligned}$$

Using this approach, it is possible to calculate what the rates of return on a stock should be if a given event did not occur. For instance, assume again that the alpha for a stock is 3 percent and beta is 2. Predicted rates of return for a given week could then be arrived at, if the market rates of return are known.

Assume that a market average exists, and that the daily averages for the week in question are:

Monday	210
Tuesday	230
Wednesday	235
Thursday	244
Friday	242

Assume that the previous Friday's market close was 200. That Monday, the rate of return for the market would be 5 percent: (210 minus 200 divided by 200). Approximate holding period rates of return could be calculated for each day.

Monday	5%	
Tuesday	10%	(230 − 210)/210
Wednesday	2%	(235 − 230)/230
Thursday	4%	(244 − 235)/235
Friday	−1%	(242 − 244)/244

For purposes of simplicity, all numbers were rounded up to the nearest percent.

Predicted rates of return for the stock in question could then be calculated using the formula previously discussed: $r_x = a + b(r_m)$

Monday	13%:3 + 2(5)
Tuesday	23%:3 + 2(10)
Wednesday	7%:3 + 2(2)
Thursday	11%:3 + 2(4)
Friday	1%:3 + 2(−.1)

Suppose that the actual rates of return for the stock in question are known. For instance:

Monday	15%
Tuesday	27%
Wednesday	10%
Thursday	11%
Friday	6%

Then the actual versus predicted returns could be compared. The residual shows the above (or below) normal returns that would accrue to stockholders of this stock, perhaps due to some corporate event.

Monday's residual would be 2 percent (15 percent minus 13 percent.) Residuals for the rest of the week would appear thus (actual returns minus predicted returns):

Monday	2%
Tuesday	4%
Wednesday	3%
Thursday	0
Friday	4.6%

A cumulative residual can be calculated by summing all the daily residuals.

Monday	2%
Tuesday	6%:(2+4)
Wednesday	9%:(2+4+3)
Thursday	9%:(2+4+3+0)
Friday	13.6%:(2+4+3+0+4.6)

Assuming that over this week the impact of the event ran its course, then the cumulative residual would represent all the supernormal profits shareholders gained because that event occurred.

Assume that cumulative residuals the week before and the week after the event in question are known. The residuals from the week before are:

Monday	.5%
Tuesday	.2%
Wednesday	−.5%
Thursday	−.2%
Friday	12%

and from the week after:

Monday	13%
Tuesday	10%
Wednesday	9%
Thursday	5%
Friday	1%

Using this information, and information previously calculated for the event week, a graph showing the cumulative residuals over time could be drawn and is shown in Figure 5.1.

This graph clearly shows the impact of the event. The Friday before, news may have leaked out and caused a big jump in actual returns over predicted returns. By Friday of the week after the event week, the impact appears to have just about run its course. Whether or not the event is significant has to be tested statistically.

Event studies show that daily returns, rather than weekly or monthly

Figure 5.1
Cumulative Average Residuals

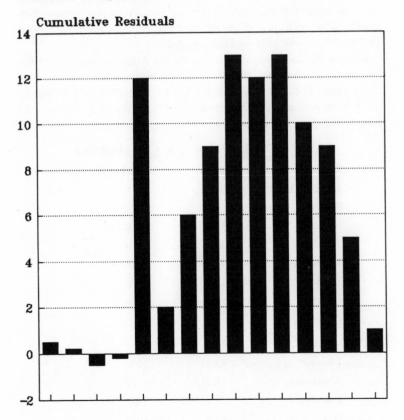

Cumulative Residuals

Days

returns, are best for showing the impact of an event. There are different approaches used by different researchers for going about crunching these numbers. The bibliography at the end of this chapter lists some references for learning more about event methodology. Appendices two and three to this chapter reprint some articles covering practical and philosophical notions of event studies.

EXAMPLE OF EVENT METHODOLOGY

Suppose someone wanted to test the impact of an event that occurred on April 1. It would be necessary to calculate firm alpha and beta. It would be wisest to go back for some time, say for one quarter, before the event to do so. (Many researchers go back 180 days before an event.) For this example, it will be simpler to just assume three months, four weeks in each month, and five trading days in each week. The first week will start on Monday, January 1.

Assume the following data exists for the company and the market. For an actual company, dividends should be included in holding period returns. If they are paid at the end of a quarter, they should actually be amortized over the period. Again, for the sake of simplicity, assume this company pays no dividends.

DAILY QUOTES: STOCK X AND MARKET

Day	Price	Market Average
JANUARY		
Week 1		
Monday	13.5	1000
Tuesday	13.5	1001
Wednesday	13.75	1015
Thursday	12.75	1013
Friday	14	1036
Week 2		
Monday	13	1032
Tuesday	13.25	1036
Wednesday	13.375	1038
Thursday	13.5	1032
Friday	13.5	1033

Day	Price	Market Average
JANUARY		
Week 3		
Monday	13.75	1040
Tuesday	13.75	1041
Wednesday	13.5	1035
Thursday	14.5	1040
Friday	15	1045
Week 4		
Monday	15.25	1050
Tuesday	14.75	1045
Wednesday	15.25	1054
Thursday	15.25	1051
Friday	16	1060
FEBRUARY		
Week 1		
Monday	16.75	1070
Tuesday	16	1059
Wednesday	15.75	1055
Thursday	18	1090
Friday	18	1062
Week 2		
Monday	16.25	1075
Tuesday	16.375	1090
Wednesday	16.5	1095
Thursday	15	1069
Friday	14.75	1060
Week 3		
Monday	15.25	1070
Tuesday	15.375	1076
Wednesday	15.5	1078

DAILY QUOTES: STOCK X AND MARKET (Continued)

Day	Price	Market Average
FEBRUARY		
Week 3		
Thursday	15.75	1087
Friday	16	1095
Week 4		
Monday	16.25	1097
Tuesday	16	1095
Wednesday	16.25	1090
Thursday	15	1090
Friday	16.75	1093
MARCH		
Week 1		
Monday	17	1095
Tuesday	16.75	1100
Wednesday	16.5	1090
Thursday	17	1090
Friday	17	1093
Week 2		
Monday	17.25	1095
Tuesday	17.25	1096
Wednesday	17.5	1097
Thursday	17.125	1090
Friday	17.5	1100
Week 3		
Monday	17.75	1103
Tuesday	17.75	1105
Wednesday	16.75	1102
Thursday	17.75	1111
Friday	17.5	1110

Day	Price	Market Average
MARCH		
Week 4		
Monday	17.75	1118
Tuesday	18	1119
Wednesday	17.75	1118
Thursday	16.75	1115
Friday	17	1123

Using the holding period return formula, daily returns for Stock X and the market may be calculated.

DAILY RETURNS: STOCK X AND MARKET

Day	Stock X	Market
JANUARY		
Week 1		
Monday	0.00	0.00
Tuesday	0.00	0.10
Wednesday	1.85	1.40
Thursday	−7.27	−0.20
Friday	9.80	2.27
Week 2		
Monday	−7.14	−0.39
Tuesday	1.92	0.39
Wednesday	0.94	0.19
Thursday	0.93	−0.58
Friday	0.00	0.10
Week 3		
Monday	1.85	0.68
Tuesday	0.00	0.10
Wednesday	−1.82	−0.58
Thursday	7.41	0.48
Friday	3.45	0.48

DAILY RETURNS: STOCK X AND MARKET (Continued)

Day	Stock X	Market
JANUARY		
Week 4		
Monday	1.67	0.48
Tuesday	−3.28	−0.48
Wednesday	3.39	0.86
Thursday	0.00	−0.28
Friday	4.92	0.86
FEBRUARY		
Week 1		
Monday	4.69	0.94
Tuesday	−4.48	−1.03
Wednesday	−1.56	−0.38
Thursday	14.29	3.32
Friday	−12.50	−2.57
Week 2		
Monday	3.17	1.22
Tuesday	0.77	1.40
Wednesday	0.76	0.46
Thursday	−9.09	−2.37
Friday	−1.67	−0.84
Week 3		
Monday	3.39	0.94
Tuesday	0.82	0.56
Wednesday	0.81	0.19
Thursday	1.61	0.83
Friday	1.59	0.74
Week 4		
Monday	1.56	0.18
Tuesday	−1.54	−0.18

Day	Stock X	Market
FEBRUARY		
Week 4		
Wednesday	1.56	−0.46
Thursday	−7.69	0.00
Friday	11.67	0.28
MARCH		
Week 1		
Monday	1.49	0.18
Tuesday	−1.47	0.46
Wednesday	−1.49	−0.91
Thursday	3.03	0.00
Friday	0.00	0.28
Week 2		
Monday	1.47	0.18
Tuesday	0.00	0.09
Wednesday	1.45	0.09
Thursday	−2.14	−0.64
Friday	2.19	0.92
Week 3		
Monday	1.43	0.27
Tuesday	0.00	0.18
Wednesday	−5.63	−0.27
Thursday	5.97	0.82
Friday	−1.41	−0.09
Week 4		
Monday	1.43	0.72
Tuesday	1.41	0.09
Wednesday	−1.39	−0.09
Thursday	−5.63	−0.27
Friday	1.49	0.72

Calculating the regression line for the above data shows that the alpha for Stock X is minus .00107 and the beta is just about 3. Returns for Stock X could then be predicted using the following equation:

$$R_X = -.00107 + 3(R_m)$$

The market index for the second quarter appears:

MARKET INDEX: QUARTER TWO

APRIL	Wk. 1	Wk.2	Wk.3	Wk.4
Monday	1100	1120	1127	1148
Tuesday	1104	1125	1141	1149
Wednesday	1108	1128	1140	1152
Thursday	1110	1129	1143	1145
Friday	1126	1126	1145	1157

MAY	Wk. 1	Wk. 2	Wk. 3	Wk. 4
Monday	1158	1162	1158	1167
Tuesday	1160	1157	1159	1169
Wednesday	1161	1152	1168	1171
Thursday	1167	1155	1164	1165
Friday	1168	1156	1165	1170

JUNE	Wk. 1	Wk. 2	Wk. 3	Wk. 4
Monday	1172	1185	1184	1182
Tuesday	1175	1182	1187	1183
Wednesday	1173	1180	1189	1181
Thursday	1174	1186	1185	1185
Friday	1184	1185	1178	1186

Holding period returns for the market may then be calculated.

APRIL	Wk. 1	Wk.2	Wk.3	Wk.4
Monday	0.00	-0.53	0.09	0.26
Tuesday	0.36	0.45	1.24	0.09
Wednesday	0.36	0.27	-0.09	0.26
Thursday	0.18	0.09	0.26	-0.61
Friday	1.44	-0.27	0.17	1.05

MAY	Wk. 1	Wk. 2	Wk. 3	Wk. 4
Monday	0.09	-0.51	0.17	0.17
Tuesday	0.17	-0.43	0.09	0.17
Wednesday	0.09	-0.43	0.78	0.17
Thursday	0.52	0.26	-0.34	-0.51
Friday	0.09	0.09	0.09	0.43

JUNE	Wk. 1	Wk. 2	Wk. 3	Wk. 4
Monday	0.17	0.08	-0.08	0.34
Tuesday	0.26	-0.25	0.25	0.08
Wednesday	-0.17	-0.17	0.17	-0.17
Thursday	0.09	0.51	-0.34	0.34
Friday	0.85	-0.08	-0.59	0.08

Using the alpha and beta already calculated, predicted returns for Stock X for the second quarter may be calculated.

PREDICTED RETURNS

APRIL	Wk.1	Wk.2	Wk.3	Wk. 4
Monday	-0.0011	-1.59	0.27	0.78
Tuesday	1.08	1.35	3.72	0.27
Wednesday	1.08	0.81	-0.27	0.78
Thursday	0.54	0.27	0.78	-1.83
Friday	4.32	-0.82	0.51	3.15

MAY	Wk.1	Wk.2	Wk.3	Wk. 4
Monday	0.26	-1.53	0.51	0.51
Tuesday	0.51	-1.29	0.27	0.51
Wednesday	0.27	-1.29	2.34	0.51
Thursday	1.56	0.78	-1.02	-1.53
Friday	0.27	0.27	0.27	1.29

JUNE	Wk.1	Wk.2	Wk.3	Wk. 4
Monday	0.51	0.24	-0.24	1.02
Tuesday	0.77	-0.75	0.75	0.24
Wednesday	-0.51	-0.51	0.51	-0.51
Thursday	0.27	1.53	-1.02	1.02
Friday	2.55	-0.24	-1.77	0.24

Actual returns for Stock X can be generated if stock price quotes are known.

STOCK PRICES

APRIL	Wk.1	Wk.2	Wk.3	Wk. 4
Monday	23.00	27.00	22.75	22.75
Tuesday	24.75	27.75	23.00	23.00
Wednesday	25.25	23.25	23.25	23.50
Thursday	26.00	23.125	23.25	22.50
Friday	26.25	22.75	23.00	23.00

MAY	Wk.1	Wk.2	Wk.3	Wk. 4
Monday	22.75	19.00	16.00	16.25
Tuesday	19.875	19.00	16.75	16.50
Wednesday	19.00	18.00	16.50	16.25
Thursday	19.25	18.00	16.25	16.25
Friday	19.25	17.75	16.00	16.675

JUNE	Wk.1	Wk.2	Wk.3	Wk. 4
Monday	16.50	16.00	16.50	16.00
Tuesday	16.25	16.25	16.25	16.25
Wednesday	16.50	16.25	16.50	16.125
Thursday	16.25	16.50	16.75	17.50
Friday	16.75	16.25	16.25	17.25

Now returns for Stock X for the second quarter may be calculated.

APRIL	Wk. 1	Wk. 2	Wk. 3	Wk. 4
Monday	35.29	2.86	0.00	-1.09
Tuesday	7.61	2.78	1.10	1.10
Wednesday	2.02	-16.22	1.09	2.17
Thursday	2.97	-0.54	0.00	-4.26
Friday	0.96	-1.62	-1.08	2.22

MAY	Wk. 1	Wk. 2	Wk. 3	Wk. 4
Monday	-1.09	-1.30	-9.86	1.56
Tuesday	-12.64	0.00	4.69	1.54
Wednesday	-4.40	-5.26	-1.49	-1.52
Thursday	1.32	0.00	-1.52	0.00
Friday	0.00	-1.39	-1.54	2.62

JUNE	Wk. 1	Wk. 2	Wk. 3	Wk. 4
Monday	-1.05	-4.48	1.54	-1.54
Tuesday	-1.52	1.56	-1.52	1.56
Wednesday	1.54	0.00	1.54	-0.77
Thursday	-1.52	1.54	1.52	8.53
Friday	3.08	-1.52	-2.99	-1.43

Residuals and cumulative residuals for each day may be calculated.

APRIL

	Week 1		Week 2	
Day	Residual	Cumulative	Residual	Cumulative
Monday	35.29		4.45	46.29
Tuesday	6.53	41.82	1.43	47.72
Wednesday	0.94	42.76	-17.03	30.69
Thursday	2.43	45.19	-.80	29.88
Friday	-3.36	41.84	-.81	29.07

	Week 3		Week 4	
Day	Residual	Cumulative	Residual	Cumulative
Monday	-0.26	28.80	-1.87	23.31
Tuesday	-2.62	26.18	.83	24.14
Wednesday	1.36	27.54	1.39	25.54
Thursday	-0.78	26.76	-2.42	23.11
Friday	-1.58	25.18	.93	22.18

MAY

	Week 1		Week 2	
Day	Residual	Cumulative	Residual	Cumulative
Monday	-1.36	20.83	.23	2.73
Tuesday	-13.15	7.68	1.29	4.02
Wednesday	-4.67	3.01	-3.97	0.05
Thursday	-0.24	2.77	-0.77	-0.72
Friday	-0.27	2.49	-1.65	-2.39

	Week 3		Week 4	
Day	Residual	Cumulative	Residual	Cumulative
Monday	-10.37	-12.75	1.05	-13.42
Tuesday	4.42	-8.34	1.03	-12.39
Wednesday	-3.83	-12.17	-2.02	-14.41

Day	Week 3		Week 4	
	Residual	Cumulative	Residual	Cumulative
Thursday	-.49	-12.66	1.53	-12.88
Friday	-1.81	-14.47	1.33	-11.55

JUNE

Day	Week 1		Week 2	
	Residual	Cumulative	Residual	Cumulative
Monday	-1.56	-13.11	-4.72	-19.33
Tuesday	-2.29	-15.40	2.31	-17.01
Wednesday	2.05	-13.36	0.51	-16.50
Thursday	-1.78	-15.14	0.01	-16.49
Friday	0.53	-14.61	-1.27	-17.77

Day	Week 3		Week 4	
	Residual	Cumulative	Residual	Cumulative
Monday	1.78	-15.99	-2.56	-18.46
Tuesday	-2.26	-18.25	1.32	-17.13
Wednesday	1.03	-17.22	-0.26	-17.39
Thursday	2.54	-14.69	7.51	-9.88
Friday	-1.21	-15.90	-1.67	-11.55

From these figures, a graph may be drawn plotting the cumulative residuals, as shown in Figure 5.2.

Figure 5.2
Cumulative Residuals over Time

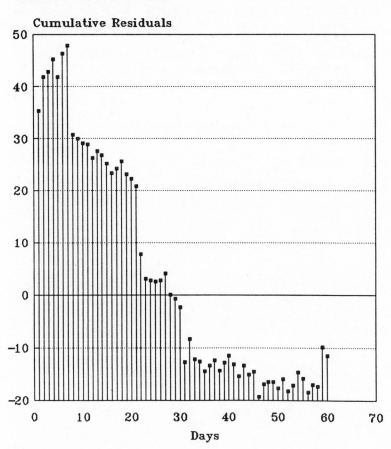

Cumulative Residuals

Days

REFERENCES

Brown, K. C., Lockwood, L. J., and Lummer, S. L. "An Examination of Event Dependency and Structural Change in Security Pricing Models." *Journal of Financial and Quantitative Analysis* (September 1985), pp. 315–334.

Brown, S., and Warner, J. B. "Measuring Security Price Performance." *Journal of Financial Economics* (September 1980), pp. 205–258.

Brown, S., and Warner, J. B. "Using Daily Stock Returns in Event Studies." *Journal of Financial Economics* (March 1985), pp. 3–31.

Fama, E. F., Fisher, L., Jensen, M., and Roll, R. "The Adjustment of Stock Prices to New Information." *International Economic Review* (February 1969), pp. 1–21.

Peterson, Pamela. "Event Studies: A Review of Issues and Methodology." *Quarterly Journal of Business and Economics* (Summer 1989), pp. 36–65.

Appendix 5.1: Methodological Approaches to Security Price Valuation

This study tests the effectiveness of two different methodologies for measuring security price movements resulting from public announcements: the Cumulative Prediction Error (CPE) and the Market Model Residual (MMR) techniques. By implementing a simulation approach, normal and abnormal stock returns are generated to test the validities of each methodology. Overall results indicate that the CPE technique does not appear to provide an accurate measurement of security performance. However, the MMR technique contains an acceptable level of precision for purposes of evaluating abnormal returns. The validity of the CPE technique demands further analysis before more substantive conclusions can be drawn.

INTRODUCTION

Extensive research has been performed in the area of capital market pricing since Eugene Fama presented the efficient market theory in 1970. While empirical results have consistently supported the weak form of the Efficient Market Hypothesis (EMH), studies on the semistrong and strong forms of the EMH appear to yield contradictory results. Several techniques have been developed to improve the measurement of security price performance in further testing of the semistrong form of market efficiency. One of the more commonly used methods for this purpose is the CPE technique developed by Dodd and Warner, used to detect abnormal security performance. For an interval from period T_{1j} to T_{2j}, the CPE for security j is defined as the sum of residuals (i.e., actual returns minus predicted returns) of security j for that particular interval.

Generally, the studies of the semistrong form of the EMH involve an examination of the timing and magnitude of price adjustments due to related announcements (e.g., stock splits, primary offerings, management developments, and economic news). Since the CPE technique provides insights as to both the timing and magnitude of announce-

This appendix is reprinted from Tsz W. Cheng, Carroll Aby, Jr., and T. Hillman Willis, "Methodological Approaches to Security Price Valuation," *Journal of Financial and Strategic Decisions* 1, no. 2, 1989.

ment effects, Hite and Owers and Davidson and Glascock used the CPE technique to successfully detect abnormal returns from spin-off and rerating announcements, respectively.

Rather than implementing the CPE technique to examine abnormal price performances, the thrust of this study is to evaluate its overall effectiveness. To provide a basis for comparing the relative merit of the CPE technique, the MMR approach is also tested. The MMR technique is another measure to detect abnormal performance. For a certain hypothetical event period (period O), MMR for N securities is defined as the average residual at period O.

Since the MMR method has been more widely accepted as a valid measure, the same data is applied to test both techniques simultaneously. It is then possible to determine the performance of the CPE method relative to its MMR counterpart. If the results from the tests are consistent with those of previous research, the methodology and included data should be validated.

METHODOLOGY

Sample

A random sample of 50 stocks was initially selected from a population of 400 stocks with a Value Line timeliness ranking of one or two. Average annual prices for the 50 sampled companies were collected from 1971 to 1986. The S&P 500 Index is used as a proxy for market return. Preliminary testing revealed that the values of the test statistics are not altered when performance returns are expressed on either a daily or annual basis. Although both the returns and standard deviations of annual data are greater than those of the monthly data, their test statistics are not altered much because both the MMRs and the CPEs are standardized by their standard deviations, which cause the t and Z statistics to remain generally unchanged. Consequently, annual returns are used and represent normal returns of the company, because no company can theoretically underperform or outperform the market on a consistent basis over time.

Research Structure

Actual means and standard deviations of the stock and S&P 500 returns are employed as parameters. Simulated stock and market returns are then generated from a normal distribution by employing the Box-Muller Method and the market model is adapted to predict theoretical (normal) returns. Once the residuals (prediction errors) are determined by subtracting the simulated actual returns from the simulated predicted returns, the CPE and MMR techniques are employed to calculate the respective test statistics. The MMR statistic is computed first. The same set of residuals is then used to calculate the CPE statistic. The steps are summarized below.

1. Obtain sample of company stock prices and S&P 500 index values.

2. Calculate the annual returns for each company and market.

3. Calculate the means and standard deviations for the companies and market.

4. Generate 50 simulated returns for the companies and market with the Box-Muller technique.

5. Formulate a regression function (Single Index Model) for each company.

6. Compute the simulated predicted returns.

7. Calculate the simulated residuals.

Statistical theory dictates that for a normally distributed sample of normal returns, there is a probability of α that the null hypothesis of no abnormal performance will be rejected even though the null hypothesis is true. In other words, if the inputs used are normally distributed and represent returns of normal performance, then on condition that the CPE and MMR technique provide valid measures, about 5 percent (if the α level is 0.05) of the simulated samples should lead to a wrong conclusion (i.e., concluding that there is an abnormal performance in the sample but in fact there is no abnormal performance). Therefore, by observing the percentages of replications rejected by the techniques, one can judge whether the techniques employed are valid or not. By using simulated returns, it is possible to replicate the test procedures as many times as desired to generate a steady α value for each method. This α value represents the percentage of replications leading to the conclusion of having abnormal performance when a large number of replications are employed.

A second aspect of the research is to test the sensitivity of the two techniques by introducing artificial abnormal returns in the data set. The entire procedure is repeated when varying the levels of these abnormal returns and then recording the number of rejected hypotheses to determine how effectively the techniques can detect abnormal performance.

Annual returns for the 50 randomly selected companies are calculated by averaging the annual high and low prices and incorporating this value in:

$$R_{jt} = \frac{P_{jt} - P_{j,t-1}}{P_{j,t-1}} \times 100 \qquad \text{(Equation 1)}$$

where R_{jt} represents the return for company j $(1-50)$ at time t $(1-16)$. After R_j is computed a geometric mean for each company is calculated with:

$$G_j = [\pi R_{jt}]^{1/16} \qquad \text{(Equation 2)}$$

Standard deviations for each company are determined with:

$$\text{STD } (R_{jt}) = \frac{[\Sigma \ R_{jt} - R_j]^{1/2}}{16 - 1} \qquad \text{(Equation 3)}$$

The same procedures are employed in arriving at the mean return and standard deviation for the market.

To simulate normally distributed returns, the Box-Muller process generator technique is used. This method uses:

$$V_t = (-2\text{Ln}[r1])^{1/2} \times \cos \ (6.28 \ [r2]) \qquad \text{(Equation 4)}$$

$$SR_{jt} = \overline{R}_j + \text{STD } (R_j) \times V_t \qquad \text{(Equation 5)}$$

where

r1,r2 = random numbers

V_t = normally distributed variate at time t

SR_{jt} = simulated return for the company j at time t

$\overline{R}_j$ = mean return for the company j

$STD(R_j)$ = standard deviation for the company j

By the same token, simulated market returns can be generated in the manner:

$$SMR_t = \overline{MR} + STD(MR) \times V_t \qquad \text{(Equation 6)}$$

where

SMR_t = simulated market return at time t
$\overline{MR}$ = mean market return
$STD(MR)$ = standard deviation for market return

For the purpose of formulating regression functions for the 50 simulated companies, 45 returns for the market and each company are first generated. For each simulated company, the first 25 simulated returns are used in the estimation of regression parameters, while the remaining 20 returns are used to calculate the predicted returns. The reason for choosing 45 simulated returns is mainly a compromise between accuracy of the regression parameters estimated and computational efficiency. The same reason applies to the choice of using 25 returns for regression and 20 returns for prediction. The numbers reflect an ample sample size for the central limit theorem to apply.

The market model is basically a regression model as follows:

$$NR_{jt} = \alpha_j + \beta_j R_{mt} + \epsilon_{jt} \qquad \text{(Equation 7)}$$

where

NR_{jt} = normal return on security j at time t
R_{mt} = market return at time t
ϵ_{jt} = random error for security j at time t

The coefficients α_j and β_j are the regression parameters of the intercept and the slope for security j, respectively. For the estimation period, the first 25 simulated market and company returns are used to compute the parameter estimates (α_j and β_j). Then the remaining 20 simulated market returns are employed to estimate 20 predicted returns (PR_{jt}) for each company. Table 5.1 summarizes the variables for both regression and prediction periods.

Table 5.1

Substituted Variables for the Regression and Prediction Periods

	REGRESSION	PREDICTION
Time Period (t)	1 to 25	26 to 45
Original Model Variables:		
NR_{jt}	SR_{jt}	PR_{jt}
R_{mt}	SMR_t	SMR_t
Unknown	α_j, β_j	PR_{jt}

The predicted return (PR_{jt}) for each company is defined as:

$$PR_{jt} = \alpha_j + \beta_j \, SMR_t \qquad \text{(Equation 8)}$$

where

PR_{jt} = predicted returns on security j at time t (t = 26 to 45)
α_j, β_j = parameter estimates for intercept and slope respectively
SMR_t = simulated market return at time t (t = 26 to 45)

The prediction error (or residual) for security j at time t (PE_{jt}) is calculated as:

$$PE_{jt} = SR_{jt} - PR_{jt} \qquad \text{(Equation 9)}$$

The CPE Technique

The CPE for each security j from period T_{1j} to T_{2j} is defined as:

$$CPE_j = \sum_{t=T_{1j}}^{T_{2j}} PE_{jt} \qquad \text{(Equation 10)}$$

The Cumulative Average Residual (CAR) for a sample of N securities is:

$$CAR = \sum_{j=1}^{N} CPE_j \: / \: N \qquad \text{(Equation 11)}$$

In this study, T_{1j} and T_{2j} are 26 and 45 respectively, while N is equal to 50.

Under the condition of normal performance, the expected value of CAR will be zero. The test statistic used is:

$$Z = \sum_{j=1}^{N} MSCPE_j \: / \: N^{1/2} \qquad \text{(Equation 12)}$$

where

$$MSCPE_j = \sum_{t=T_{1j}}^{T_{2j}} SPE_{jt} \: / \: (T_{2j} - T_{1j} + 1)^{1/2}$$

where

$T_{2j} - T_{1j} + 1 = $ the number of days in the test period.
(In this case, $T_{2j} - T_{1j} + 1 = 20$.)

and

$$SPE_{jt} = PE_{jt} \: / \: S_{jt} \qquad \text{(Equation 13)}$$

The SPE_{jt} and Z are unit normal in the absence of abnormal performance. S_{jt} is the estimated standard deviation. The standard deviation for security j at time t is given by:

$$S_{jt} = [S_j^2 \left(1 + \frac{1}{D_j} + \frac{(SMR_t - \overline{SMR})^2}{\sum\limits_{t=1}^{D_j}(SMR_t - \overline{SMR})^2} \right)]^{1/2} \quad \text{(Equation 14)}$$

where

S_j = residual variance for security j

D_j = number of observations during the regression period (D_j = 20)

SMR_j = simulated market return at time j of the prediction period

SMR_t = simulated market return at time t of the prediction period

$\overline{SMR}$ = average simulated market return

The MMR Technique

In the case of any given security, the MMR technique uses the average residual (AR_o) at the hypothetical event period O as the performance measure:

$$AR_0 = \frac{1}{N} \sum_{j=1}^{N} PE_{j0}$$ (Equation 15)

where

PE_{jo} = prediction error (or residual) for security j at time period O

The test statistic (t*) is given by:

$$t^* = \frac{AR_0}{\frac{1}{N}\left[\sum_{j=1}^{N}\left(\frac{1}{D_j-2}\sum_{t=1}^{D_j}\left[PE_{jt}-\left(\sum_{t=1}^{D_j}\frac{PE_{jt}}{D_j}\right)\right]^2\right)\right]^{1/2}}$$

(Equation 16)

where

N = number of securities (N = 50)

D_j = number of observations during the regression period (D_j = 20)

PE_{jt} = prediction error for security j at time t

The statistic is t-distributed with (D_{j-1}) degrees of freedom for the assumed normal and independent residuals.

Detecting Abnormal Performance

To check the effectiveness of both techniques in detecting abnormal performance, artificial abnormal returns are added to the simulated returns (SR_{jt}) at a predetermined time period t1 for each security. The introduced abnormal returns are 10 percent, 15 percent, and 20 percent. In these cases, the higher the percentage of the replications rejecting the null hypothesis, the better the method should be.

FINDINGS

The percentage of rejections for the test of the null hypothesis that there is no abnormal performance is reported in Table 5.2 and Table

Table 5.2
Rejection Rates for the MMR Technique

Actual Levels of Abnormal Performances (Two-Tail Test)	Rejection Rates (RR)	
	$\alpha = 5\%$	$\alpha = 1\%$
0%	$\|t*\| \geq 2.1$ N = 150 RR = 2.63%	$\|t*\| \geq 2.86$ N = 150 RR = 0.67%
10%	$\|t*\| \geq 1.73$ N = 125 RR = 53.20%	$\|t*\| \geq 2.54$ N = 125 RR = 27.00%
15%	$\|t*\| \geq 1.73$ N = 100 RR = 81.60%	$\|t*\| \geq 2.54$ N = 100 RR = 66.30%

Table 5.3
Rejection Rates for the CPE Technique

Actual Levels of Abnormal Performances (Two–Tail Test)	Rejection Rates (RR)	
	$\alpha = 5\%$	$\alpha = 1\%$
0%	$\|Z^*\| \geq 1.96$ N = 375 RR = 10.00%	$\|Z^*\| \geq 2.58$ N = 375 RR = 4.00%
20%	$\|Z^*\| \geq 1.65$ N = 100 RR = 28.00%	$\|Z^*\| \geq 2.33$ N = 100 RR = 8.00%

5.3. For the MMR technique (see Table 5.2), tests are conducted at both the 5 percent and 1 percent significance levels. Normal performance denotes an abnormal performance of zero percent. The MMR test is replicated 150 times. If the absolute value of t is greater than or equal to 2.10 (for 5 percent level) or 2.86 (for 1 percent level), abnormal performance is considered to exist in the sample. Since there are ordinarily no abnormal returns, the MMR test should reject the null hypothesis for the percentage of times equal to the percentage of the chosen significance level. For the test at the 5 percent level, the rejection rate is 2.63 percent, while the rate is 0.67 percent at the 1 percent level. Since the two rejection rates are less than the levels of significance, the MMR tests do not reject often enough to conclude abnormal returns.

Two levels of abnormal returns were introduced to the MMR technique. A 10 percent return added to a single time period of a company implies an increase of only 0.5 percent on the average. Yet 53.2 percent of the tests became significant at the 5 percent level. A larger increase is noted at the 1 percent level (from 0.67 percent to 27 percent). For the 15 percent added return level, 81.60 percent and 66.30 percent of the replications are significant at the 5 percent and 1 percent levels respectively.

The rejection rate for the CPE method (Table 5.3) at the 5 percent level reaches 10 percent, which is twice the correct limit and for the 1 percent level there is a 4 percent rejection rate or four times the limit. Since 375 replications were made, the sample was considered to be large enough to reach a steady state.

By examining the actual Z statistics, a great variability exists in the set of Z scores. Among the 38 significant Z values (i.e., about 10 percent of 375 replications), more than 40 percent of them exceed the critical value of 2.58, which suggests a tendency to generate extreme values. Thus, a sample of stocks with normal returns may easily be mislabelled with abnormal performance under the CPE technique.

While the CPE technique does not perform well under conditions of normal performance data, results are more unsatisfactory as abnormal returns are introduced. Under the 20 percent abnormal performance level, the CPE test detects only 28 cases out of 100 replications at 5 percent level. For the 1 percent level, eight observations out of 100 are determined to be significant. These rejection rates are in fact lower than the percentages for the MMR tests, which suggest that the CPE test does not indicate abnormal performances as efficiently.

CONCLUSION

It is difficult to validate whether the simulation approach is a proper way to test the techniques, or if the normally distributed simulated returns are good estimates of their real world counterparts. The actual grand mean return for the sample is 11.5 percent, while the standard deviation is 33 percent. These figures are about one-third higher than the market averages for the last few decades, but as the residuals are standardized by some ways in both techniques, the magnitude of the inputs should not significantly affect the results. For the replications of no normal performance, the rejection rate of the MMR tests is too low while that of the CPE tests is too high. This indicates that the research methodology and the data set being used can at least provide results in both directions (i.e., greater or smaller than the correct level). A similar study by Brown and Warner found a rejection rate of 4.4 percent for the MMR tests. So, if this methodology really understates the rejection frequencies, then the rejection rates for the CPE tests should then be even higher.

The primary benefit of this study provides explanatory evidence for the potential dangers of using the CPE and MMR techniques. Certainly, the CPE test suffers more problems than the MMR tests. Besides rejecting too many null hypotheses, insensitivity to abnormal returns is another major deficiency. On the other hand, the MMR test appears to pick up the abnormal returns more efficiently. At this stage a concrete conclusion would not be appropriate. More levels of abnormal performance need to be introduced in the models to check the corresponding changes in the rejection rates.

REFERENCES

Box, G.E.P., and Muller, M. E. "A Note on the Generation of Random Normal Deviates." *Annuals of Mathematical Statistics* 29, pp. 610–611.

Brown, Stephen J, and Warner, Jerald B. "Measuring Security Price Performance." *Journal of Financial Economics* (September 1980), pp. 205–258.

Davidson, Wallace N., III, and Glascock, John L. "The Announcement Effects of Preferred Stock Re-ratings." *Journal of Financial Research* (Winter 1985), pp. 317–325.

Dodd, P., and Warner, J. "On Corporate Governance: A Study of Proxy Contests." *Journal of Financial Economics* (April 1983), pp. 401–438.

Fama, Eugene F. "Efficiency and Capital Markets: A Review of Theory and Empirical Work." *Journal of Finance* 25 (May 1970), pp. 383–417.

Hite, Gailen L., and Owers, James E. "Security Price Reactions around Corporate Spin off Announcements." *Journal of Financial Economics* (December, 1983).

Reilly, Frank K. *Investment Analysis and Portfolio Management*. New York: CBS College Publishing, 1985.

Watson, Hugh J. *Computer Simulation in Business*. New York: John Wiley & Sons, Inc., 1981.

Appendix 5.2: Experimental Designs in Event Study Methodologies

INTRODUCTION

As a general statistical approach, Event Study Methodologies (ESM) are the most generally applied empirical techniques in financial literature. They are now widely used to test competing and alternative hypotheses. Application history dates back to Fama, Fisher, Jensen and Roll (1969) in their classic study regarding the adjustment of stock prices to new information. However, basic return-generating norms may be traced back to the works of Markowitz (1959) and Sharpe (1963), an era that marked the inception of the modern theory of finance. An increasing number of works in various areas of finance and financial economics have been predicated on the empirical content of their research base and this class of methodologies. Simulation experiments using ESM and sensitivity analysis are also widespread. An examination of event study methodologies indicates that a distinctive field of research has evolved from these simulation studies. Some recent works using ESM include Brown and Warner (1985), Michel and Shaked (1984), Dyckman, et al. (1984), Fields and Schelor (1985), and Davidson and Glascock (1985) The importance of this class of methodologies cannot be overstated. For the first time a methodology is in fact crossing from finance to economics and other fields. The crossovers include such distant fields as cleometrics (cf., Marshall, 1985). There are options to event study methodologies. However, most alternative methods lack the degree or size of the information impact (e.g., size of abnormality of returns) and cannot be quantitatively measured relative to the pre-event condition.[1] Furthermore, other methods do not incorporate core configurations, such as the market model. They in turn lack the forcefulness of the event study methodologies.

Applications of event study methodologies include such items as market efficiency and abnormal returns, stock splits, take-overs and anti–take-overs, and speeds of adjustment and response. Also included are unusual occurrences (such as the Three Mile Island accident), proxy contests, deregulation impacts, and announcement effects, such as

This appendix is reprinted from Carroll Aby, Jr., and Heydar Pourian, "Experimental Designs in Event Study Methodology," *Journal of Financial and Strategic Decisions* 1, no. 2, 1989.

changes in ratings, among others.[2] Most often, an event study concerns the impact of new information on one or more variables of primary interest.

A survey of literature reveals that there are numerous issues involved in ESM. The purpose of this study is to selectively present a critical review of experimental designs contained in ESM research. Each of these programs use various but distinctly recognizable classes of event study methodologies. The survey is focused on the works that have more recently contributed to several areas of finance, financial economics, and accounting literature.

An overview of ESM is presented in the following section. Its main thrust is interpreted from a generalized experimental design. This section also includes a sketch of the dominant Markowitz-Sharpe return-generating model and variations on the ESM theme. In the next section, different problematic "event conditions" are discussed: event-date uncertainty, the role of portfolio size, and the magnitude of information impact. Insofar as time aggregation is concerned, the final section contains a discussion of the data. The paper concludes with some suggested research programs on this class of methodologies. Included are focuses on the distribution of event-time uncertainty and "parsimony" in modeling and estimation.

EXPERIMENTAL DESIGNS

There are a variety of experimental designs in the financial and accounting literature. In the following diagram an attempt is made to generalize those found in the literature. The steps common in designing an event study experiment include the following.

Determination of the Event Date

The event date occurs when the impact of information is presumed to have occurred. However, the event-date need not be known precisely (see below). Nevertheless, the preciseness of the event-date remains one of the problematic areas of ESM.

Selection of an Estimation Period

The estimation period is defined as the time when the parameters of the selected model are estimated by use of the ordinary least squares method. Other methods, such as the Scholes-Williams risk-estimation technique, are also used.

Analytically, the estimation period can be divided into two parts. The first can be referred to as the pre-event estimation period, and the second the post-event estimation period. Most of the works in finance use the pre-event period for estimation. This implicitly assumes that the impact of information during and after the event is a one-time, permanent affair, and that there would be no need to continue the test period beyond the event period.

Once the post-event period is explicitly considered, the estimated parameters of the model are based on both pre- and post-event periods. If this approach is selected, then the study presupposes that the impact of information is temporary and occurs during the event period. If the focus is on measuring the impact of temporary information, then the use of both pre- and post-event periods for estimation periods is justified. However, if measuring the impact of a continuing phenomenon, then the parameters of the model need to be estimated only on the basis of the pre-event period observations.

Fama et al.'s (1969) work was initially the most prominent application of ESM. However, its basic market model formulation stems from a work of Markowitz (1959) with Sharpe's elaboration (1963). If rewritten in the error term, this model is common to most ESM studies in the following format:

$$U_{it} = R_{it} - (\alpha_i + \beta_i \times R_{mt}) \qquad \text{(Eq. 1)}$$

where

U_{it} = the prediction error

R_{it} = actual return on security i at date t

R_{mt} = the market factor at date t

α_i, β_i = firm specific OLS estimated parameters

During the last several years, researchers have encountered various problems associated with tests of financial hypotheses. This has been particularly serious with regard to the level of securities trading. As a result, more variations on the theme of event study methodologies have been developed. The basic variations of the fundamental market model include: (1) Mean-Adjusted Returns Model, (2) Market-Adjusted Returns Model, (3) Market Model with Scholes-Williams beta-estimation procedure being equivalent to using an instrumental variable (1977), and (4) Market Model with Dimson beta-estimation procedure with aggregated coefficients (1979).

The Mean Adjusted Returns Model sets the a_i in Equation 1 to the average return for firm i over the estimation period. Thus:

$$U_{it} = R_{it} - \tilde{R}_i \qquad \text{(Eq. 2)}$$

where

$\tilde{R}_i$ is designated as the mean. If generalized,
$\tilde{R}_i$ will take the following formulation:

$$\tilde{R}_i = (1/n) \, \Sigma \, R_{it}, \, (t = -g \, . \, . \, . -h, \, h \, . \, . \, .m) \qquad \text{(Eq. 3)}$$

where $n = (g - 2h + m + 2)$ and Σ is used as the summation sign. In this model β_i is set equal to zero. Insofar as simplicity is concerned, this model is the most naive.[3]

In the Market-Adjusted Returns Model, $\alpha_i = 0$ and $\beta_i = 1$. Thus, the market model simplifies as follows:

$$U_{it} = R_{it} - R_{mt} \qquad \text{(Eq. 4)}$$

The basic market model relies on the traditionally estimated α_i and β_i, since these two parameters are estimated by using the ordinary least squares method. However, in the Scholes-Williams model (1977), beta is estimated through an equivalent instrumental variable approach for nonsynchronous data. (See Figure 5.3.)

$$\alpha_i = (1/n) \, [\Sigma \, R_{it} - \beta_{it} \times \Sigma \, R_{mt}], \, (t = -g. \, . \, . -h, \, h. \, . \, .m) \text{ (Eq. 5)}$$

and

$$\beta_{it} = (\beta'_i + \beta''_i) \div (1 + 2G) \qquad \text{(Eq. 6)}$$

Figure 5.3
An Exhibit of Alternative Experimental Designs and an h-Period Event Date Uncertainty

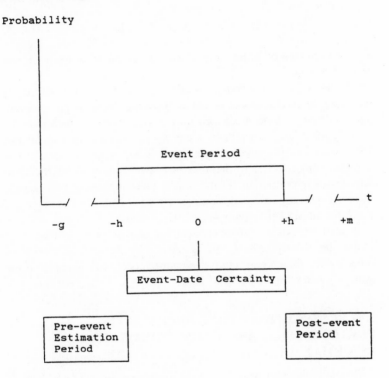

Probability

Event Period

Event-Date Certainty

Pre-event
Estimation
Period

Post-event
Period

Assigned Uniform Probabilities:

$$P(\text{Odd-Day}) = 1 / (2h + 1)$$

$$P(\text{Even-Day}) = 1 / 2h$$

Timing of the primed betas is computed with respect to R_m for time $(t-1)$ lag and $(t+1)$ lead, respectively. G_m is the estimated first-order market autocorrelation coefficient.

Finally, the market model can be coupled with Dimson aggregated coefficients estimation procedure (1979). In this next procedure, as in Scholes-Williams:

$$\alpha_i = (1/n) \ [\Sigma \ R_{it} - B_{it} \times \Sigma \ R_{mt}], \ (t = -g. \ . \ . \ -h, \ h \ . \ . \ .m) \quad \text{(Eq. 7)}$$

but

$$\beta'_{it} = \Sigma \ \beta_{ik}, \ (k = -h. \ . \ .h) \qquad \text{(Eq. 8)}$$

β_{ik} are estimated by ordinary least squares (OLS) for a given lag and lead, such as h.[4]

The use of each method is based on a set of critical assumptions regarding the market processes and asset pricing. For example, an event study is by definition predicated on a "base event," which must be initially identified. In addition, a comparable event must parallel this base event. In this sense, an event study is a conditional method. The application of conclusions that may be drawn from the study therefore requires extreme caution. In the future, other models may be added. This is especially true if the proposed model evolves in the spirit of the Efficient Market Hypothesis (EMH).

Analytically, the dominant presumption of event study methodology is that the underlying process is generated by the selected model. In other words, the chosen return-generating model is assumed to fit the general assumption of the ESM.

EVENT CONDITIONS: DATE UNCERTAINTY, PORTFOLIO SIZE, AND MAGNITUDE OF THE INFORMATION IMPACT

Generally there are at least three characteristics related to each event that defines an ESM: existence of event-date uncertainty, effect of portfolio size, and magnitude of the impact of information on the variable under investigation.[5] In turn, these event conditions have a degree of interdependency, as discussed later in this section.

In an event study, the researcher is generally confronted with at least three issues regarding the event condition. The first, when does the innovation (in the statistical sense) occur? Alternatively, when is the announcement made, or when is the relevant information released? A related concern is whether or not the researcher can identify with certainty the inception of news. If the answer to the last question is yes, then the event date can be specified precisely at $t = 0$, a condition which can be referred to as event date certainty. Similarly, event date uncertainty can be defined as the uncertainty over a given length of time during which the event is presumed to or could have occurred. In the case of event date uncertainty, the procedure is often to assign implicit probabilities as dictated by a uniform probability distribution. Analytically, however, one could design a different probability distribution in such a way that the most certain date gets the greatest probability of being the event date. As opposed to the certainty of an event date such as Three Mile Island, many other events are not so well defined. An example is the effect of a deregulation. Yet, the specification of a precise event date is rather critical to an event study methodology (cf., especially, Dodd et al., 1984). Intuitively, the precision of event date is imperative.

Event date uncertainty takes its toll on research programs concerned with detecting abnormal returns—the dominant subject of ESM. The more uncertain the occurrence of the event or event date, the less successful will be the proof of the hypothesis involved in the study. For example, suppose that the thrust of a study is the detection of abnormal returns on the share price of a firm or group of firms within an industry on a daily basis. Further, assume that the researcher is uncertain about the occurrence of an event. The question arises, then, as how to deal with such an event date uncertainty.

The researcher can generally choose among two alternatives: (1) selecting a two-day or longer event date uncertainty specification, or (2) ignoring the uncertainty and choosing a one-day event date. There appears to be a trade-off between these alternatives. The longer the event date uncertainty, the less minimizing the probability of Type I error related to the hypothesis under investigation. On the other hand, choosing the wrong event date under uncertainty could naturally damage the expected results. As the number of dates of the event span increases, detecting the impact of new information (e.g., abnormal returns) becomes more difficult. In other words, the abnormality by definition is supposed to have occurred precisely at the unknown event date. Therefore, the pre- and post-event date inclusion, which then includes normal returns patterns, makes it difficult to detect the abnormal returns during the two-day event date and longer.

From a positive view, however, the correct statistical inference in regard to the hypothesis under investigation with event date uncertainty appears to be reachable. From a classical statistical theory, it appears that a researcher should choose the first alternative given above.

Figure 5.4
Probability of Success of Detecting the Correct Impact of Information

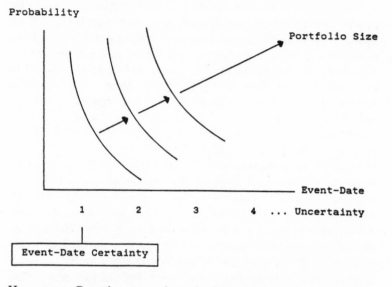

However, a Bayesian researcher who incorporates the *a priori* judgment may select choice two.[6] If the first choice is selected, there is often a need for maturity-matching beta estimation in the following sense. If a two-day event date uncertainty is included in the study, then the beta should probably be estimated over two days rather than over daily data (cf., e.g., DeAngelo and Rice, 1983). In other words, when the precision of event date is lacking and the researcher would like to avoid *a priori* specification of a one-day event, then the multi-day estimation approach should be used.

Portfolio size is another event condition issue. The literature generally reveals that the larger the portfolio size, the larger the probability of success of the hypothesis under investigation. This may be due to the fact that larger portfolios compensate for the nonnormal distribution often discovered in time-disaggregated (such as daily) data.

Finally, the outcome and results of any event study depend on the magnitude of the variable's deviation from the norm under focus. Naturally, the larger the deviations, the larger the probability of successfully detecting the impact of information under investigation. This implies that small deviations from the norm do not make good event studies. The relation of these two event conditions is exhibited through Figure 5.4.

CONCLUSIONS AND IMPLICATIONS FOR FURTHER RESEARCH

Several conclusions may be drawn from a survey of the literature, a few rather uncontroversial. The accomplishments of an event study will be positively related to (1) precision in the specification of the event date, (2) size of abnormality subject to detection, and (3) portfolio size. Among these conditions, the event date uncertainty appears to be the most troublesome factor observed in current research programs. The larger the uncertainty of the event date, the less the chance of statistical detection of abnormality, *ceteris paribus*.

While more time-disaggregated data will not entirely solve the event date uncertainty, it will help to approach the precision of the event date specification. This is consistent with Brown and Warner's observation that there are "substantial gains to more precise pinpointing of an event" (1985, p. 12). It seems proper to suggest that researchers should use more time-disaggregated data in event study applications. There appears to be no difficulty that would inhibit an event study using more time-disaggregated data.

On the other hand, specifying the variety of market model does not appear to be an important factor in an event study. For instance, models with the traditionally computed beta appear to perform equally well as those with more specialized betas, such as Scholes-Williams or Dimson Betas. Dychman et al., show that more sophisticated methods of estimating risk do not enhance the ability to detect the impact of new information (1984, p. 21). The results of various studies appear to be in line with modern econometrics (e.g., Zellner, 1980) and time series analysis (e.g., Box and Jenkins, 1970), which emphasize parsimony in modeling and estimation.

Several issues remain for further research. These include: (1) the continuous event (e.g., deregulation) versus a one-time event (e.g., stock split); (2) the effect of the size of abnormality in returns and the significance of an event study; (3) theoretical research on the probability approach to specification of event date in case of uncertainty; (4) Single-period versus multiperiod estimation procedures (when event uncertainty exists); (5) eliminating difficulties introduced by nonsynchronous trading through other beta estimation procedures; and (6) insight into the unsettled nature of variance over the event period, especially around the event date.

Finally, there is a need to study basic alternative return-generating models in actual situations and not necessarily in simulations. These alternatives may include the Fama-MacBeth (1973 and 1976, p. 348) approach. Insofar as the estimation is concerned, it appears that use of ARIMA modeling to identify and estimate the autocorrelation structure of returns during the event period may be appropriate.

NOTES

1. Two widely used alternatives to event study methodology are the regression technique, using dummy variables (see, e.g., Barrett et. al., 1986), and the intervention analysis developed by Box and Tiao (1970).

2. For related studies see the reference section.

3. Benesh and Brown show that mean-adjusted returns model and the market model will produce similar residuals when mean return on the market over the period used to estimate the market model parameters equals the return on the market in event time t (1985, p. 7).

4. The lead and lag in Dimson procedure need not coincide with the interval of the event period.

5. Other event conditions discussed in the literature include event date clustering and risk clustering (cf., Brown and Warner, 1980).

6. For an advocate of the use of Bayesian statistical approach, see e.g, Aeller (1981).

REFERENCES

Aharony, J., and Swary, I. "Quarterly Dividend and Earnings Announcements and Stockholders' Returns: An Empirical Analysis." *Journal of Finance* (March 1980).

Barrett, W. B., et al. "The Effect of Three Mile Island on Utility Bond Risk Premia: A Note." *Journal of Finance* (March 1986), pp. 255–61.

Benesh, G. A., and Brown, S. L. "On the Irrelevance of Slope Coefficients in Studies of Market Efficiency." *The Financial Review Proceedings* 20 (August 1985), p. 7.

Box, G.E.P., and Tia, G. C. "Intervention Analysis with Applications to Economic and Environmental Problems." *Journal of the American Statistical Association* 70 (March 1970), pp. 70–79.

Brown, S. J., and Warner, J. B. "Measuring Security Price Performance." *Journal of Financial Economics* 8 (Sept. 1980), pp. 205–58.

Brown, S. J., and Warner, J. B. "Using Daily Stock Returns: The Case of Event Studies." *Journal of Financial Economics* 14 (March 1985), pp. 3–31.

Davidson, W. N., III, and Glascock, J. L. "The Announcement Effects of Preferred Stock Re-Ratings." *Journal of Financial Research* 8 (Winter 1985), pp. 317–25.

DeAngelo, H., and Rice, R. "Antitakeover Charter Amendments and Stockholder Wealth." *Journal of Financial Economics* 7 (June 1979) pp. 3–31.

Dimson, E. "Risk Measurements When Shares Are Subject to Infrequent Trading." *Journal of Financial Economics* (June 1979), pp. 197–226.

Dodd, P. "Merger Proposals, Management Discretion and Stockholder Wealth." *Journal of Financial Economics* 8 (June 1980).

Dodd P., et al. "Qualified Audit Opinions and Stock Prices: Information Content, Announcement Dates and Concurrent Disclosures." *Journal of Accounting and Economics* 5 (April 1984), pp. 3–38.

Dyckman, T., Philbrick, D., and Stephan, J. "A Comparison of Event Study Methodologies Using Daily Stock Returns: A Simulation Approach." *Journal of Accounting Research* 22, Supplement (1984), pp. 1–30.

Fama, E. F. "Portfolio Analysis in a Stable Paretian Market." *Management Science* 11 (January 1965), pp. 404–19.

———. "The Behavior of Stock Market Prices." *Journal of Business* 11 (January 1965), pp. 34–105.

Fama, E., Fisher, L., Jenson, M., and Roll, R. "The Adjustment of Stock Prices to New Information." *International Economic Review* 10 (February 1969), pp. 1–21.

Fama E. F., and Macbeth, J. D. "Risk, Return and Equilibrium: Empirical Tests." *Journal of Political Economy* 71 (May-June 1973), pp. 607–33.

Fama, E. F., and Miller, M. H. *The Theory of Finance.* Hinsdale, Ill.: Dryden Press, 1972.

Fields, A., and Shelor, G. "Press Date as a Valid Representative of Announcement Date in Merger Research." Southern Finance Association, Dallas, November 1985.

Garven, J. R., and Vora, G. "Unanticipated Information and Its Intra-Industry Effects: A Case-Study of the Union Carbide Mishap." Presented at FMA meetings, Denver, October 1985.

Henderson, G. V., Jr., Glascock, J. L., Officer, D. T., and Shaw, V. "A Note on the Event-Time Form of Residual Analysis." Southern Finance Association, Dallas, November 1985.

Kaplan, R., and Roll, R. "Investor Evaluation of Accounting Information: Some Empirical Evidence." *Journal of Business* 18 (April 1972), pp. 225–57.

Katz, S., et al. "Stock Market Behavior around Distress and Recovery Predictions from Bankruptcy Models." Working paper, Baruch-CUNY, 1984.

Klein, A., and Rosenfeld, J. "The Influence of Market Conditions on Event Study Residuals Using the Mean Adjusted Returns Model." Southern Finance Association, Dallas, November 1985.

Markowitz, H. M. *Portfolio Selection: Efficient Diversification of Investments.* New Haven, CT: Yale University Press, 1959.

Marshall, R. "Tutorial on Event Study Methodologies." Southern Finance Association, Dallas, November 1985.

Michel, A., and Shaked, I. "Airline Performance under Deregulation: The Shareholder's Perspective." *Financial Management* 13 (Summer 1984), pp. 5–14.

Mukherjee, T. K. "Stock Price Behavior Surrounding Proxy Fights for Control: A Non Parametric Approach." *Review of Business and Economic Research* (Fall 1985), pp. 85–103.

Patell, J., and Wolfson, M. "The Ex Ante and Ex Post Price Effects of Quarterly Earnings Announcements Reflected in Opinions and Stock Prices." *Journal of Accounting Research* (Autumn 1981), pp. 434–58.

Patell, J., and Wolfson, M. "Good News, Bad News, and the Intraday Timing of Corporate Disclosures." *The Accounting Review* (July 1982, pp. 509–27.

Rogers, R. C., and Owers, J. E. "Equity for Debt Exchanges and Stockholder Wealth." *Financial Management* 14 (Autumn 1985), pp. 18–26.

Scholes, M., and Williams, J. "Estimating Betas from Nonsynchronous Data." *Journal of Financial Economics* (December 1977), pp. 309–27.

Schwert, G. W. "Using Financial Data to Measure Effects of Regulation." *Journal of Law and Economics* 24 (April 1981), pp. 121–58.

Sharpe, W. F. "A Simplified Model for Portfolio Analysis." *Management Science* (January 1973).

Zellner, A. "Philosophy and Objectives of Econometrics." Invited Paper for British Association of University Teachers of Economics, Durham, England, March 1980.

6

Proxy Fights

When a corporation is organized, it files articles of incorporation or a corporate charter with appropriate state authorities. The ownership of the company, referred to as stock in the company, is described. The owners of the stock in the company have certain rights, among them voting rights. Companies often have two classes of stock, one voting and one nonvoting. The voting rights of most corporations are cumulative, meaning that one vote is granted for each share of stock owned. That, of course, means that corporations are not democracies where everyone would be equally represented, but that larger stock owners wield more power in managing the corporation.

Charter changes and voting for the board of directors occurs at annual meetings. Shareholders may attend the meetings, or they may instead allow someone else to cast their vote for them by proxy. Management generally solicits proxies from shareholders and casts votes for them. From time to time, though, warring factions attempt to wrest control of a firm from the incumbent management through proxy fights.

Proxy fights are sometimes bitter, protracted, and expensive to the company. Often proxy fights are for the representation of a differing viewpoint, or to highlight a special issue. Some proxy fights have been initiated by stockholders attempting to block company business with

South Africa. Some have been all-out battles to win directors' positions and thus control the company. Some have been fought in hostile take-overs.

Proxy fights have become big business. There are in fact proxy solicitors, who take on corporate giants. Don Carter was a premier proxy solicitor. His services were retained when Saul Steinberg decided to take on the Disney enterprises in a giant take-over attempt. Carter snatched a six-figure fee, even thought the proxy fight was never initiated. He commands a 68-person staff, including private detectives.

The casual observer may wonder just what kind of damage a proxy fight can do to a company. Considering the legal haranguing, negative publicity, and time lost in combat, it would be easy to jump to the conclusion that proxy fights have a devastating impact on corporations. Some academic researchers have examined the impact of proxy fights on firm stock price.

WEALTH IMPACTS ON STOCK PRICE

Dodd and Warner examined the price behavior of firms that were the target of proxy fights. They studied 96 firms that had experienced proxy contests for control between July 1, 1962, and January 31, 1978. Using the traditional event study methodology, they found evidence of a significant positive abnormal return, from 59 days prior to the announcement of a proxy fight, all the way to the announcement of resolution. Perhaps most interesting, and probably astounding, is that Dodd and Warner found this positive abnormal return to exist no matter what the outcome of the fight. Whether the company lost some control or whether it won, stockholders actually benefited from a proxy fight.

In a later study, Mukherjee also examined the impact of proxy fights on stock price over three periods prior to the announcement of a proxy contest, from the date of announcement to the result date, to the period after resolution. His sample, unlike that of Dodd and Warner, focused only on contests for control. Using the *Wall Street Journal* index as a source, he identified 95 companies that were involved in contests for control between 1964 and 1982.

Mukherjee used a different approach than that of Dodd and Warner. He relied on nonparametric tests (sign, Chi-square, and Wilcoxon tests) instead of traditional event methodology. By doing so, he thought he avoided some of the drawbacks of the event approach. What he found, though, was perhaps surprising. Just as Dodd and Warner found, there is evidence of positive stock performance associated with proxy fights. Instead of stopping at these general findings, he went a few steps further and made several interesting observations:

1. Positive abnormal performance was evident in the preannouncement period, sometimes as much as six months before.

2. During the period between the announcement and resolution, however, the companies involved in proxy fights suffered. Findings further indicated that companies that had unsuccessful contests had worse performance than the sample as a whole. Mukherjee stated it seemed evident that the market anticipated which companies were to be involved in unsuccessful contests. Mukherjee defined an unsuccessful contest as one in which the dissident group lost.

3. In the postresolution period, sample firms outperformed the market index firms.

The results of both these studies, therefore, are somewhat startling. Rather than tear companies apart, proxy fights may actually benefit shareholders. Mukherjee even reveals some investment strategies that may be used in light of his findings. For instance, an investor may short stocks involved in proxy fights on the day of announcement. Then, for a short-term investment, an investor might buy back stocks in companies after proxy fights have been resolved.

REFERENCES

Dodd, Peter, and Warner, Jerold. "On Corporate Governance: A Study of Proxy Contests." *Journal of Financial Economics* (April 1983), pp. 401–38.

Mukherjee, Tarun K. "Stock Price Behavior Surrounding Proxy Fights For Control: A Non-Parametric Approach." *Review of Business and Economic Research* (Fall 1985), pp. 85–103.

Sherrid, Pamela. "Fighting Dirty." *Forbes* (September 10, 1984), pp. 190–91.

7

Dividends, Stock Splits, and Repurchases

Dividends are not hard to understand. Corporate owners want a share of the profits their firm generates. If a corporation does make profits, it has two choices: either pay them out to owners in the form of dividends, or plow them back into the company (retained earnings). Of course, many firms opt to combine the two.

This chapter is devoted to dividends—the dividend decision, the mechanics of dividends, forms of dividends, and the wealth impact of dividends—as well as stock splits and repurchases.

As already stated, dividends are corporate profits divided among owners of a corporation. A firm decides to pay dividends based on such factors as legal and contractual constraints and liquidity position. The company also recognizes that investors may want periodic returns on their investment, in the form of dividends.

MECHANICS

Corporate dividends are paid on the vote of the board of directors. Most U.S. companies pay dividends quarterly. The board decides the amount and form of dividend, when the list of shareholders eligible to receive dividend payments is to be drawn (record date), and when the dividends are actually to be paid.

To allow time for record keeping, four business days prior to the record date is the ex-dividend date. Any stocks sold during the ex-dividend period will be sold without rights to the current dividend. The actual dividend payment date is usually two to three weeks after the date of record.

METHOD OF PAYMENT

Dividend payments may be in the form of cash, merchandise, or stocks. If in cash, the company will usually cut the checks in-house or contract with a third party (generally a bank or trust company) to handle the dividend process.

Occasionally, companies have resorted to merchandise dividends. This usually occurs only when a company is suffering financial distress. Generally, shareholders are not too pleased to receive merchandise dividends. The company may even do more harm by this than foregoing the dividend by sending messages of financial distress to the market.

Companies may also declare stock dividends. For example, assume during the quarterly board meeting, the directors declare a 10 percent stock dividend. For every ten shares of stock, shareholders will receive another share. Naive stockholders might also assume that their wealth position will increase by 10 percent. Unfortunately, such is not the case. Essentially, each stockholder owns the same percentage of the company as before, regardless of whether that stockholder has ten or eleven pieces of paper. If the company's value is the same after the stock dividend as before, then the only thing that has really changed is the number of stock certificates. The market is aware of the true impact of the stock dividend and adjusts the market price per share accordingly. The impact of a stock dividend on shareholder wealth, then, is nil.

WEALTH IMPACT OF DIVIDENDS

Theoretically, investors should be indifferent between receiving a cash dividend or having stock appreciate in value because profits are plowed back into the company, assuming transaction costs are covered. Certainly, tax implications might play a part, but with the Tax Reform Act of 1986 capital gains taxes were eliminated, and taxes on capital gains and dividends are now equivalent.

The evidence, albeit weak evidence, especially that reported since the Tax Reform Act (Aharony and Swary, 1980; Charest, 1978; Eades et al., 1984) suggests that investors do prefer dividends over capital gains. Some have suggested that this is due to an information effect (Bhattacharya; 1979; Ross, 1977), which postulates that managers send information about future directions of the company by raising, or not cutting, dividends. The evidence supporting this notion is not clear, however.

The ex-dividend behavior of stocks has been studied. It might be reasonable to assume that stock prices should decline by the amount of the declared dividend on the ex-dividend date. Evidence, again weak, suggests that such is not the case, however (Campbell and Beranek, 1955; Durand and May, 1960; Elton and Gruber, 1970).

STOCK SPLITS

Stock splits, closely related to dividend policy, simply involve increasing the number of shares of stock in a company. For instance, consider the case of a hypothetical company with the following data.

HYPOTHETICAL, INC.

Common stock outstanding:	1,000,000 shares
Par value per share:	$1
Market price per share:	$100
Dividend pay-out ratio:	40%
Net income:	$1,000,000

Several observations may be made based on this data.

Earnings per share:	$1 (calculated by dividing net income [$1,000,000] by number of shares [1,000,000])
Dividends per share:	$.40 (total dividends would be calculated by multiplying the net income of $1,000,000 by the 40% dividend rate; to get dividends per share divide this total by the number of shares of 1,000,000)

Hypothetical's board of directors declares a two-for-one stock split, meaning that for every share of stock a new one will be issued. A stockholder with 20,000 shares would own 40,000 after the split. What about the impact of the split on other variables? Resultant variables would appear thus:

HYPOTHETICAL, INC.

Common stock outstanding:	2,000,000 shares
Par value per share:	$.50
Market price per share:	$50
Dividend pay-out ratio:	40%
Net income:	$1,000,000

The apparent changes are easily explained. Since there was a two-for-one split, the number of shares of common stock was doubled. In order for the common stock account on the firm's balance sheet to be accurate, then, the par value of the stock was split in half. Assets and liabilities of the firm would remain the same. Therefore, the total value of the company would remain the same. If such is the case, then the market price of the firm should be split, at least theoretically. Resultant earnings and dividends per share may be calculated.

Earnings per share:	$.50 (calculated by dividing net income [$1,000,000] by number of shares [2,000,000])
Dividends per share:	$.20 (total dividends would be calculated by multiplying the net income of $1,000,000 by the 40% dividend rate; then to get dividends per share divide this total by the number of shares of 2,000,000)

The effect on the firm's shareholders is also easy to calculate. If the market value is now $50, shareholders are in the same position as before the split. A shareholder with 20,000 shares before the split would have had a wealth position of $2,000,000 (20,000 times $100). After the split, that same shareholder will have a wealth position of $2,000,000 (40,000 times $50). Before the split, the shareholder would have received $8,000 in dividends, based on net income of $1,000,000 ($.40 dividends per share times 20,000 shares). Based on the same level of income, that shareholder would still receive $8,000 in dividends ($.20 dividends per share times 40,000 shares).

So, at least in theory, the company as well as the shareholders are no better or worse off than before the split. The rationale behind the stock split is to make stock easier to trade by bringing its market value down. The evidence may suggest something else, however.

The landmark research study in stock splits (Fama et al., 1969) concluded that the market was efficient in digesting stock split information, but recent evidence suggests otherwise. Nichols and McDonald (1983) reported that stocks of companies with moderate changes in corporate earnings prior to a stock split were relatively efficient. Companies with large changes in corporate earnings prior to a stock split clearly experienced abnormal price behavior. Grinblatt, Masulis and Titman (1984) reported that stock splits generated positive abnormal returns of nearly 3 percent on the date of announcement of a split. Ohlson and Penman (1985) in a study of stock splits found that stock volatilities increase significantly during the split period. All in all, recent studies seem to fly in the face of traditional thought and should prove fodder for future research efforts.

STOCK REPURCHASES

Stock repurchases, also closely related to dividend policy, occur when a company buys back its own stock to either retire the stock or hold it as treasury stock, either through a tender offer or purchase in the secondary markets. There are a number of reasons a firm might wish to repurchase its own stock: (1) as an anti–take-over measure, (2) to reduce future cash dividend requirements, (3) to use for stock option plans or employee stock purchase plans, (4) to invest excess cash, (5) to bolster market price. The last reason requires some explanation. Assume the following facts about Hypothetical:

Market price per share:	$10
Shares of stock outstanding:	1,000,000
Net income:	$1,000,000

Hypothetical therefore has an earnings per share of one dollar ($1,000,000 of net income divided by 1,000,000 shares of outstanding stock). The price-earnings ratio for the company's common stock would be ten (market price per share of ten dollars divided by earnings per share of one dollar).

Assume Hypothetical buys up 20 percent of its outstanding common stock. Pertinent information would appear thus:

Shares of stock outstanding: 800,000
Net income: $1,000,000

Earnings per share would then be $1.25 ($1,000,000 net income divided by 800,000 shares of stock outstanding). If the same price-earnings ratio of ten applied, then Hypothetical's market price per share should jump to $12.50. Should this price-earnings ratio hold, though? Theoretically, perhaps not. If the total value of the company has not changed, then the aggregate market value should be the same as before the repurchase, regardless of the number of shares of stock outstanding. The evidence regarding stock repurchases suggests otherwise.

In an early study of repurchasing activity, Dann (1981) found significant positive returns accruing to shareholders of repurchasing companies within one day of the repurchase announcement. Even more startling, Dann found that these positive returns were permanent, in that they did not return to preannouncement levels following the repurchase date.

Dann further found evidence that wealth changes are also realized by owners of convertible debt securities and convertible preferred stock. Dann attributed these effects to an information effect. He hypothesized that the repurchase announcement conveyed favorable new information regarding the firm's future prospects. However, Dann concluded that the specific nature of information conveyed to stockholders is not readily apparent.

The same year, Vermaelen published a study using event methodology. Vermaelen studied 131 firms that repurchased their stock during 1962–77, and found that the average positive residual for sample firms was 23 percent.

Asquith and Mullins (1983) studied the puzzle of dividends and repurchases, and cited three possible reasons for repurchases:

1. Investor tax argument. Repurchases are favored over dividends if capital gains taxes are due on repurchases, but ordinary taxes are due on dividends. (This advantage disappears if no capital gains tax exists, however).
2. Leverage hypothesis. Through repurchases of common stock, a firm can alter its capital structure, increase its debt ratio, and thereby reap benefits of higher leverage.

3. Some have suggested that firms merely repurchase stock based on recommendations of investment bankers, who have a vested interest in repurchase activity.

Davidson and Garrison (1989) studied repurchasing behavior and likewise found positive effects of repurchases. Dividing their sample into various subsamples, they found that the larger the repurchase as a percentage of total stock outstanding, the greater the effect. Firms that repurchased more than 18 percent of their outstanding stock had larger residuals than those repurchasing less than 18 percent.

The authors also examined the stated reason for repurchase. They found that firms that purchased stock to prevent take-overs had negative reactions. On the other hand, if companies cited attempting to enhance stock value as the reason for repurchase, the impact was quite positive. They also examined the financing for the repurchase and found that those companies with large decreases in current ratios and increases in debt ratios experienced negative impacts upon announcement of a repurchase.

REFERENCES

Aharony, J., and Swary, I. "Quarterly Dividend and Earnings Announcements and Stockholders' Returns." *Journal of Finance* (March 1980), pp. 1–12.

Asquith, P., and Mullins, D. "The Impact of Initiating Dividend Payments on Shareholders' Wealth." *Journal of Business* 29 (Jan. 1983), pp. 77–95.

Bhattacharya, S. "Imperfect Information, Dividend Policy, and the 'Bird in the Hand' Fallacy." *Bell Journal of Economics* (Spring 1979), pp. 259–70.

Campbell, J. A., and Beranek, W. "Stock Price Behavior on Ex-Dividend Dates." *Journal of Finance* (December 1955), pp. 425–429.

Charest, G. "Dividend Information, Stock Returns and Market Efficiency." *Journal of Financial Economics* (June 1978), pp. 297–330.

Dann, Larry. "Common Stock Repurchases: An Analysis of Returns to Bondholders and Stockholders." *Journal of Financial Economics* (June 1981), pp. 113–18.

Davidson, W., and Garrison, Sharon. "The Stock Market Reaction to Significant Tender Offer Repurchases of Stock: Size and Purpose Perspective." *The Financial Review* 1 (February 1989), pp. 93–107.

Durand, D., and May, A. "The Ex-dividend Behavior of American Telephone and Telegraph Stock." *Journal of Finance* (March 1960), pp. 19–31.

Eades, K. M., Hess, P. J., and Kim, E. H. "On Interpreting Security Returns during the Ex-Dividend Period." *Journal of Financial Economics* 13 (1984), pp. 3–34.

Elton, E. J., and Gruber, M. J. "Marginal Stockholder Tax Rates and the Clientele Effect." *Review of Economics and Statistics* (February 1970), pp. 68–74.

Fama, E. F., Fisher, L., Jensen, M. D., and Roll, R. "The Adjustment of Stock Prices to New Information." *International Economic Review* 10 (1969), pp. 1–21.

Grinblatt, M. S., Masulis, R. W., and Titman, S. "The Valuation Effects of Stock Splits and Stock Dividends." *Journal of Financial Economics* 13 (1984), pp. 461–90.

Nichols, W. D., and McDonald, Bill. "Stock Splits and Market Anomalies." *The Financial Review* (November 1983), pp. 237–56.

Ohlson, J. A., and Penman, S. H. "Volatility Increases Subsequent to Stock Splits." *Journal of Financial Economics* 14 (1985), pp. 251–66.

Ross, S. A. "The Determination of Financial Structure: The Incentive-Signalling Approach." *Bell Journal of Economics* (Spring 1977), pp. 23–40.

Vermaelen, T. "Common Stock Repurchases and Market Signalling: An Empirical Study." *Journal of Financial Economics* (June 1981), pp. 139–183.

8

Death and Dissolution

KEY EXECUTIVE DEATH

Lee Iacocca of Chrysler Corporation is a notable corporate leader who is dynamic, charismatic, and has made a difference to his company, indeed to the whole automobile industry. When he took the helm of Chrysler, the company was on the brink of disaster, poised to become the largest bankruptcy to date. Instead, the company turned around, and Iacocca's leadership has been praised as the primary cause.

It would take no great imagination, therefore, to assume that, should Iacocca suddenly be absent from the picture, Chrysler might suffer.

On the other hand, many firms are saddled with leadership that actually hinders them. Take, for example, a company with a founder and former owner at the controls. The chief executive officer (CEO) might once have been vital, but is no longer even viable.

What would happen to each company should its CEO die? It is not unreasonable to assume that the death of a key executive might affect a firm's stock price. To that end, a number of researchers have looked at death and resultant effect on firm stock price.

Key Executive Death and Firm Stock Price

In 1985, Johnson et al. (1985) studied 53 sudden deaths of CEOs reported in the *Wall Street Journal* index between 1971 and 1982. The researchers reported little impact on average stock returns following the death of a key executive. They examined factors such as age, status as a corporate founder, and years employed by the firm, and found some excess returns. The executive's status as a founder was positively related, and position in the decision-making hierarchy was negatively associated with excess returns. The combination of poor performance and large shareholdings was associated with greater excess returns.

Etebari, et al. (1987) used the *Wall Street Journal* index to study a sample of 48 CEO deaths from January 1, 1972, through December 31, 1982. Three types of sudden deaths were determined, ranked in order of frequency as heart attacks, accidents, and suicides.

The average age of CEOs at the time of their deaths was determined to be 60. The authors concluded that stock market reactions to sudden deaths of CEOs were somewhat mixed. Generally, there were negative stock market reactions on the day of death, but ensuing behavior varied. For instance, in the case of deaths of board chairs there were positive cumulative returns reported over the thirty deaths subsequent to death. The authors also reported positive cumulative returns for accidental death, but no clear-cut results for death by heart attack and suicide.

In a later study, Worrell et al. (1986) studied the impact of key executive death on shareholder wealth. The authors also noted the positive cumulative returns surrounding the death of a chair only, as did Etebari et al. (1987), leading to the interesting conclusion that the market may be waiting for an antiquated figurehead to exit the stage. By monitoring the health of chairs, then, the possibility of short-term stock price gains exists. They did find negative returns associated with the death of the CEO only, however. Further, they found that name recognition made a difference. If the executive had been in the news recently, or if the name of the executive was in the name of the company, the negative impact of death was more pronounced.

Worrell and Davidson also looked at management succession after the death of a CEO, and found that market reaction was positive to the announcement of an internal successor, but not so with the announcement of an external successor. The authors conclude that rapid announcements of successors are critical, and that firms should identify and groom potential successors to key management positions.

BANKRUPTCY

When a firm falls into financial distress, the slide is usually protracted and painful and often played out in the press. When Braniff failed, not once but twice, stories appeared repeatedly in the media, up to the declaration of bankruptcy. Each succeeding story must have had some impact on firm stock price. It must be remembered, however, that even after filing, the firm's stock price still survives. It is not eliminated until final dissolution by a bankruptcy judge. The attached appendix illustrates what happens to a stock price after filing for bankruptcy. The authors Chandy and Choi (1988) find, as have previous researchers, that progressive deterioration in stock price occurs up to a bankruptcy filing, and that large losses over the two-day interval surrounding a bankruptcy filing announcement are to be expected.

REFERENCES

Chandy, P., and Choi, I. "The Effect of Bankruptcy on Stock Returns." *Journal of Financial and Strategic Decisions* 1, no. 1, (1988).

Etebari, A., Horrigan, J., and Landwehr, J. "To Be or Not to Be: Reaction of Stock Returns to Sudden Deaths of Corporate Chief Executive Officers." *Journal of Business Finance and Accounting* (Summer 1987), pp. 255–78.

Johnson, B., Magee, R., Nagarajan, N., and Newman, H. "An Analysis of the Stock Price Reaction to Sudden Executive Deaths." *Journal of Accounting and Economics* 7 (1985), pp. 151–74.

Worrell, D. and Davidson, W. N. "The Effect of CEO Succession on Stockholder Wealth in Large Firms Following the Death of the Predecessor." *Journal of Management* 13, no. 3 (Fall 1987), pp. 509–15.

Worrell, D. L., Davidson, W. N., Garrison, S. H., and Chandy, P. R. "Management Turnover through Key Executive Death: Its Effect on Investor Wealth." *Academy of Management Journal* (December 1986), pp. 674–94.

Appendix 8.1: The Effect of Bankruptcy Filings on Stock Returns

INTRODUCTION

Most corporate bankruptcy studies have focused on the ability to predict firm failure using accounting data (i.e., various financial ratios). Recently, an approach that estimates the probability of corporate failure using capital market data has been suggested. This method assumes that market expectation about changes in probability of bankruptcy should be reflected in market risk-return measures in the Capital Asset Pricing Model (CAPM) framework (Aharony et al., 1980). It has been shown that shareholders experience abnormal losses over periods of from four to six years prior to bankruptcy filing (Aharony et al., 1980), however, the effect of bankruptcy announcements at the date of filing has received little attention. This may be due to the belief that, prior to actual bankruptcy, the corporation's demise is so fully anticipated that no new information is released when bankruptcy filing does occur (Altman, 1969; Clark and Weinstein, 1983).

Aharony et al. (1980) showed that shareholders experience abnormal losses over periods of from four to six years prior to bankruptcy filing, indicating that the market anticipated impaired earnings and financial distress. In addition, it is plausible that a bankruptcy declaration signals a change in the actual probability of bankruptcy. Possibly, once bankruptcy is declared, shareholders will increasingly focus on the probability that the shares will become worthless. If so, the subsequent increase in expected value of bankruptcy costs will affect the value and risk of the bankrupt shares, leading to significant decreases in stock returns. Altman (1969) found that shareholders suffered an average capital loss of about 26 percent during the period from one month before to one month after bankruptcy announcements. Clark and Weinstein (1983) similarly showed a continuous deterioration in returns prior to and surrounding the filing date.

The purpose of this study is to demonstrate that formal bankruptcy filing contains important unanticipated information on share returns of bankrupt firms. This research also affects two other areas of study

This appendix is reprinted from P. R. Chandy and In Suk Choi, "The Effect of Bankruptcy Filing on Stock Returns," *Journal of Financial and Strategic Decisions* 1, no. 1, 1988.

using capital market data: empirical measurement of indirect cost of bankruptcy and market risk of bankrupt shares.

DATA

Organizations filing for reorganization under Chapter 11 of the Federal Bankruptcy Act from 1979 to 1983, as appeared in the *Wall Street Journal,* were used in this study. All stock returns were calculated using the Center for Research on Security Prices' (CRSP) daily return files, which include all New York Stock Exchange (NYSE) and American Exchange (AMEX) listed firms. Out of the 41 firms initially selected for study, eleven were eliminated due to the halt of trading at least 30 days prior to their filing date.

METHODOLOGY

The methodology presented by Fama et al. (1969), used to examine the behavior of the bankrupt firms, allows one to estimate a residual return (the difference between the actual return and the estimated return over an interval surrounding the event date) while using some model (i.e., the market model). The residual returns are then averaged across all companies for each event time. The average abnormal return in a given event time (AR) is given as follows:

$$ARt = \frac{1}{N} \sum_{j=1}^{N} Ejt$$

where

N = number of companies

t = event time relative to event date O (Event time O is the date in which the new information is obtained.)

Another statistic, Cumulative Average Residual (CAR), accumulates ARs over time and is computed as follows:

$$CAR = \sum_{t=1}^{T} ARt$$

where

T = number of time periods being summed

D = the total number of time periods in the sample

In this study, the event, T = 0, is the date that reorganization filing first appeared in the *Wall Street Journal*. T is equal to 187 days, that is, the trading period from 180 days before to seven days after the filing date.

Previous studies have shown that large shareholder losses prior to formal bankruptcy announcements do occur, implying that the market has reflected this information, with the announcement itself not conveying any new information to the market (Aharony et al., 1980; Altman, 1969; Clark and Weinstein, 1983). The hypothesis is that it is possible to incur additional large losses after the bankruptcy is formally declared, and that the eventual halt in trading (i.e., within seven days after the event date) may provide additional information to the market. In other words, the lesser the possibility that trading will be halted, the smaller the decrease in returns.

RESULTS

Performance measures for the stocks of the 30 filing companies are reported in Table 8.1. Both AR and CAR show an ongoing erosion of share returns during the period from event time −180 through −2. The CAR indicates a loss of about 36 percent, which is consistent with previous studies (Aharony et al., 1980; Altman, 1969). This continuous deterioration in share returns as bankruptcy approaches appears as no surprise to the market, since most corporate bankruptcies are fully anticipated.

The sharp decline in share returns before the filing date indicates that bankruptcy filing does convey information to the market. As demonstrated in Table 8.1, the AR dropped to −.145 one day before filing (T = −1) and to −.239 on the event date (T = 0). The CAR, plotted in Figure 8.1, shows the extent of drift in abnormal returns from 180 before to seven days after the event date. The CAR is −.216 on T = −2, with an accelerated downward drift reaching −.60 on the day of the event date. As indicated in Table 8.1, the ARs for T = −1 and T = 0 are significantly different from 0 at the .05 level, indicating that shareholders suffered significant additional losses in the two-day interval from T = −1 to T = 0.

Table 8.1
Daily Abnormal and Cumulative Returns

Event Time	Abnormal Returns	t Values	Cumulative AR
-180	-.003	- .069	-.003
- 90	.006	.115	.013
- 30	.015	.282	-.030
- 10	.004	.087	-.070
- 5	-.039	- .756	-.158
- 4	.001	.032	-.157
- 3	-.063	-1.261	-.220
- 2	.004	.093	-.216
- 1	-.145	-2.919*	-.360
0	-.239	-4.818*	-.600
1	-.030	- .594	-.630
2	.025	.521	-.605
3	.064	1.311	-.541
4	.001	.018	-.541
5	.025	.511	-.516
6	.022	.436	-.494
7	-.003	- .067	-.497

*Significant at .05 level

The result is consistent with that of the study by Clark and Weinstein (1983), which used a monthly return sample of 50 bankrupt stocks
for the 1938–79 period and 148 companies with daily returns data for
the 1962–79 period. According to their results, in terms of daily returns during the period from event time −220 through event time −2,
the CAR indicates a loss of .32 and over the three-day interval in
event time the change in CAR is −.47. In summary, the market re-

Figure 8.1
Cumulative Residuals

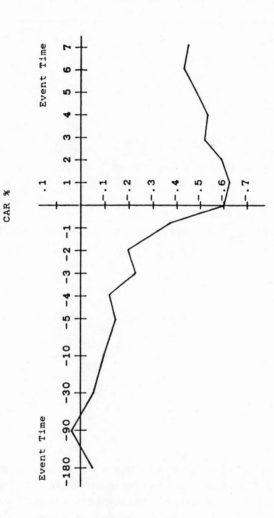

acted to the filing announcement, indicating that a bankruptcy declaration conveyed important unanticipated information to the market.

Further examination of the data reveals that instead of the expected
negative AR values after the event date, there are succeeding positive
values (except for $T = 1$). The positive values indicate reversed behavior of share returns, which may be attributed to the market's atti-
tude toward risk of the bankrupt shares.

In order to examine postreturn behavior of the bankrupt shares, the
ARs of two groups are compared. The first group contained companies
in which trading of stock was halted (i.e., over a seven-day interval
after the event date), and the other group was comprised of companies
whose shares continued to trade. If the market takes into account the
trading difference between the two groups, one can expect that the
lower the possibility that trading will be halted, the smaller the decrease in AR (or the larger the increase in AR), and vice versa. The
results are shown in Table 8.2 and Figure 8.2.

The group with no halting in trade (six firms) exhibits smaller increases in AR, while the other group in which trading was halted (13

Table 8.2
Postevent Return Behavior of Two Groups

	AR		CAR	
Event Time	Halted	Non-Halted	Halted	Non-Halted
− 2	.0254	.0005	−.0790	−.1340
− 1	−.1400	−.0850	−.2190	−.2180
0	−.2650	−.1170	−.4830	−.3350
1	−.0480	−.0680	−.5320	−.4030
2	.0090	.0600	−.5230	−.3430
3	.0890	.0170	−.4340	−.3260
4	.0150	−.0260	−.4200	−.3530
5	.0350	.0700	−.3850	−.3460
6	.0260	.0130	−.3590	−.3330
7	−.0080	.0060	−.3670	−.3270

Figure 8.2
Residuals: Halted and Nonhalted Trading

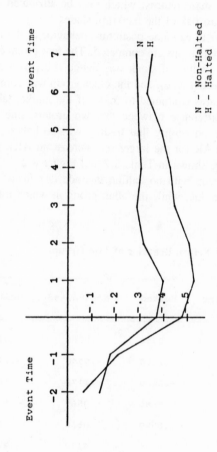

companies) shows larger increase in AR. It is difficult to explain why the return behavior of the two groups showed such unanticipated results. One possibility is that it is not appropriate to test the halting effect with such a small sample size. The other is that it is beyond the market's ability to predict the possibility for future trading of bankrupt shares, because the decision is solely made by the exchange authorities.

CONCLUSION

The market's response to the bankruptcy filing of thirty corporations over the period from 1979 to 1983 has been examined in this study. Performance measures of the bankrupt shares were computed employing the standard residual methodology. Results indicate, as found with earlier studies, that losses occur over a long period prior to formal bankruptcy filing, and that large losses can be expected over the two-day interval surrounding the event date. It can be concluded from these results that bankruptcy declaration conveys important unanticipated information to the market. However, the postevent behavior results are ambiguous. The limitation of this study is the small sample size due to the lack of trading around the bankruptcy filing date.

The results of this study could be applied to measuring indirect costs of bankruptcy.

REFERENCES

Aharony, J., Jones, C. P., and Swary, I. "An Analysis of Risk and Return Characteristics of Corporate Bankruptcy Using Capital Market Data." *Journal of Finance* 4 (September 1980), pp. 1001–16.

Altman, E. I. "Bankrupt Firm's Equity Securities as an Investment Alternative." *Financial Analysts Journal* 25 (July–August 1969), 129–33.

Altman, E. I., and Brenner, M. "Information Effects and Stock Market Response to Signs of Firm Deterioration." *Journal of Financial and Quantitative Analysis* 16, no. 1 (March 1981).

Clark, T. A., and Weinstein, M. I. "The Behavior of the Common Stock of Bankrupt Firms." *Journal of Finance* 38, no. 2 (May 1983), pp. 489–504.

Fama, E., Fisher, L., Jensen, M., and Roll, R. "The Adjustment of Stock Prices to New Information." *International Economic Review* 10, no. 1 (February 1969), pp. 1–21.

9

Mergers and Divestitures

Mergers and divestitures have certainly been the focus of media attention in the eighties. Perhaps because of the attention, perhaps just because of the raw numbers of such events, academic researchers also have focused on them.

MERGERS

Of all corporate events, mergers probably are the most frequently occurring and generate the most interest. Politics, intrigue, and power are all associated with the big mergers. Some notable mergers have garnered national attention, the fodder for weeks of nightly newscasts. Aside from all the hoopla, what impact do mergers really have?

This chapter examines merger trends, mechanics, and motives, and traces their impact on shareholder wealth. Some ploys to resist takeovers and their impact are also discussed.

Mechanics

Firms may grow either internally, by generating and reinvesting profits, or externally, by mergers. Mergers are combinations of two or more firms, but all the assets and claims against assets of the acquired firm are transferred to the acquiring firm. After a merger, only the acquiring firm survives as an entity.

Consolidations are two companies combined to make a completely new entity. Another method of external growth is to purchase the assets of another company, which may be achieved without changing firm ownership.

Mergers are generally achieved after negotiations between managers of the acquired and acquiring firms. Shareholders of both must approve the terms. If managers of the target firm object to the terms of the merger, the acquirer can circumvent them and go directly to the stockholders to get enough votes (proxies) for the merger. Only 51 percent of the outstanding shares are needed for approval.

Another way to acquire another firm is through a tender offer, which is an offer directly to its shareholders to directly purchase their stock. The acquiring firm may offer cash or stock, or a combination of stock and cash. Again, only 51 percent of the shareholders need to approve a tender offer.

Motives

Mergers have occurred throughout the economic history of the United States. Generally, mergers occur in cycles: at times merger activity is frenzied, at other times there are lulls. No one really knows why these cycles occur. The late eighties saw an explosion in merger activity, prompting heightened interest in pinpointing the causes. Some of the espoused motives for mergers include the desire to grow, enter new fields, diversify risk, gain competitiveness, expand product lines, use surplus funds, and gain tax advantages.

Growth

Growth is an important goal of companies. Investors base decisions on the growth of their returns. Indeed, in an earlier chapter, the value of common stock was said to be based on growth in earnings. Therefore, firms must grow, either internally or externally. In certain situations, external growth may be the only viable alternative, or the most expedient.

Lowering Financing Costs

Some firms may have used up their debt capacity. In the face of the necessity for growth and a lack of resources to fund it, a company may try to acquire companies with unused debt capacity. This might allow companies to rely on debt rather than equity sources of funding. Since debt is generally a cheaper source of funds than equity, this might in turn lower the cost of financing to the acquiring firm.

Using Surplus Funds

It is the job of every company to bring money into the firm, then invest it in return-generating uses, such as buying equipment or inventory. A firm might invest in marketable securities, or acquire interests in other firms.

Technological Gains

High-tech businesses have evolved in the 1980s, and, in many industries, companies must continually advance or die. To keep from becoming technologically obsolete, firms must either develop new technologies or acquire such technology externally.

Risk Reduction

Any business involved in generating profits faces risk. The economy may falter, products may become obsolete, inflation may eat into profits, or similar plights. To circumvent some of these risks, firms may choose to diversify activities.

Fighting Take-overs

Managers of target firms frequently resist take-overs, much of the time because they fear losing their jobs. In response to the merger wave of the 1980s, time-honored defensive strategies to avoid take-overs were employed, and some new strategies were developed.

Publicity Campaigns

Take-over targets frequently use the press to fight take-overs. Sometimes this turns into a virtual mud-slinging match. For example, in 1978 when Occidental Petroleum was attempting to take over Mead

Corporation, the rhetoric got hot and heavy. Mead tried to resist the take-over, and one of the key drafters of the resistance was Gershon Kekst, a public relations professional. Mead stockholders were beseiged with letters, advertisements, and press reports of wrongdoing by Occidental. Mead even went before the Ohio Securities Commission and charged Occidental with stock fraud.

Legal Maneuvers

Target management often files suits against bidders, mainly to buy time for other defensive strategies.

The Mead-Occidental battle was certainly an example of this. Each company filed motions in federal district courts during the skirmishing, and, as already stated, Mead tried to take the battle before the Securities Commission.

Another novel example of legal maneuvering occurred in 1982. Marshall Field and Company was the target of Carl Icahn and a group of investors. Predictably, Marshall Field hired a law firm to do battle. The defense was somewhat innovative in that the lawyers charged Icahn and his group with racketeering under an interpretation of the Federal Racketeering Influenced and Corrupt Organizations Act of 1970.

Counter Take-over

In counter take-overs, the target firm tries to turn the tables by buying the bidding firm.

Poison Pill

In a recent and popular strategy, target firms put clauses in their financial agreements that will be implemented if a take-over attempt takes place.

For instance, Charles E. Hurwitz fought, clawed, and bought his way to the top of McCulloch Oil Company. Once there, he started protecting himself from being knocked out of control by someone else. He instituted several anti–take-over amendments, some of which required stockholder actions to take place only at meetings, directors to not be removed without cause, and the board of directors, not stockholders, to call special meetings. All these measures were designed to thwart take-overs.

Becoming Private

On May 4, 1979, Houdaille Industries was to buy back its outstanding common stock at a price twice its book value. The company was the target of take-over rumors, and management, with the aid of an investors group and institutional lenders, undertook the costly defensive move of going private.

Charter Amendments

Increasingly, firms are amending their corporate charters to avoid potential take-over. For example, golden parachute clauses provide managers with irrevocable, and sometimes excessive, compensation when the company is taken over.

Sale of the Crown Jewel

This tactic involves selling a key asset in order to make a take-over target less desirable. In 1985, Revlon announced a plan to sell off approximately $250 million of its assets to defend against a hostile take-over bid by Pantry Pride.

White Knight Defense

This strategy involves the target approaching a third party to take over said target in order to avoid an unfriendly merger.

Gains from Mergers

Does anybody ever win in mergers? If they do, when do the gains occur? What impact do the strategies to fight mergers have on shareholder wealth? These and other topics have been the subject of a great deal of academic research, much of it using the event methodology described in this book.

In 1983, Jensen and Ruback (1983) summarized a great body of literature concerning the wealth impact of mergers. Shareholders of target firms in successful mergers tend to benefit even before the announcement of a merger. However, such gains are erased if the bidding turns sour, unless, of course, another suitor enters the picture.

The evidence of the wealth impact of bidding firms is not so clear. For instance, Dodd (1980), in a study of 71 successful and 80 unsuccessful mergers, concluded that bidders in either case earned abnormally negative returns. This led Dodd to conclude that any gains from mergers accrue to the shareholders of the target firms.

Other researchers, however, found evidence of gains to acquirers. Among them, Dennis and McConnell (1980), Asquith et al. (1986), and Bradley (1980). Most research centered on the preannouncement period through the date of merger. Little research exists showing the impact of postmerger firms, and that which exists is mixed.

Asquith et al. (1986) arrived at several important conclusions:

1. Mergers relay important information about a firm. The decision to acquire is evidence of a corporate strategy that stresses growth to shareholders.
2. The authors noted that the Williams Act of 1968 changed the corporate and legal environment concerning mergers. The act established various antifraud measures, provided for a minimum tender period, and required increased disclosure in measures. As a result, potential gains of mergers shifted from targets to bidders.
3. A size effect was noted. When the target was over 10 percent of the bidder's equity, gains to bidders were 4.1 percent, as opposed to 1.7 percent when the target was less than 10 percent of the bidder's equity.

Wealth Effects of Anti–take-over Strategies

Although the literature on the impact of anti–take-over strategies is not extensive, it is nonetheless interesting. As the prevalence of merger activity increases, so also will studies such as these.

Anti–take-over Charger Amendments

DeAngelo and Rice (1984) and Linn and McConnell (1983) studied the impact on stock price of companies that adopted anti–take-over amendments. No major impact on shareholder wealth was found.

Standstill Agreements

Dann and DeAngelo (1983) tried to measure the impact of standstill agreements—agreements requiring firms to quit repurchasing stock—on shareholder wealth. The study examined only 30 firms that had reached standstill agreements. The authors concluded that standstill agreements have a negative effect on stockholders of a target firm.

Summary

There is strong evidence that stockholders in target firms benefit—at least from some time before the merger announcement until the completion of the merger. Even shareholders in unsuccessful targets benefit from some time before a merger announcement until breakdown in merger talks. There is evidence, although not as compelling, that shareholders in acquiring firms benefit from merger attempts. Weak evidence shows postmerger benefits to shareholders. Finally, there is little evidence on defensive strategies to avoid mergers. What does exist suggests that if any benefits accrue from such ploys, they are to benefit managers rather than stockholders.

CORPORATE DIVESTITURES

In 1980 GAF Corporation announced that it was to put up a block of its assets for sale. These assets and businesses accounted for nearly half the company's sales volume.

From time to time, firms such as GAF decide to reduce by selling parts of their assets in order to infuse new cash flow, divest of an unprofitable venture, or any number of strategic reasons. They may achieve desired results by a sell-off, whereby they transfer assets to another company; spin-off, resulting in a separate publicly traded company; or voluntary liquidation, whereby all assets of the company are divested.

Such actions might, of course, affect shareholder wealth, a result supported by research.

Research

Hite and Owers (1983) and Miles and Rosenfeld (1983) found evidence of positive residuals surrounding spin-off announcements. Results on corporate sell-off, however, tend to be mixed.

For instance, Boudreaux (1975), Klein (1986), and Jain (1985) report positive returns from voluntary sell-offs.

Alexander et al. (1984) investigated the impact of voluntary sell-offs as well as spin-offs on firm stock price, and reached two principal conclusions: (1) the announcement of a voluntary divestiture has a slightly positive cumulative effect; and (2) divestitures tend to be announced after a period of generally negative abnormal returns.

Rosenfeld (1984) examined both sell-offs and spin-offs, and concluded that spin-offs outperformed sell-offs on the event day, and that gains to shareholders of both the selling and acquiring firms were almost identical.

Klein (1986) examined announcement effects of firms engaged in voluntary sell-offs. Klein found that the timing of the announcement had an impact on firm stock price. On average, the initial announcement of sell-off resulted in a positive excess return. When the sample was divided into subsamples, further information was gleaned. When the transaction price was announced with the initial announcement, the result was significantly positive. On the other hand, when no price was announced, there was no excess return. Klein also found that larger sell-offs tend to produce larger announcement-day responses. Subsequent announcements produced insignificant excess returns.

In a more specialized study, Tehranian et al. (1987) examined the impact of sell-offs on firm stock prices and looked at divesting companies with long-run performance plans. The researchers found that firms that compensate executives with long-run performance plans showed a significantly positive abnormal return around the announcement of a divestiture. On the other hand, firms without such compensation plans showed an insignificant negative stock market reaction.

Skantz and Marchesini (1987) examined the wealth effects of complete voluntary liquidations and reported significant positive returns. In fact, the announcement-month average excess return was 21.4 percent. Their sample only included 37 firms, however.

REFERENCES

Asquith, P., Bruner, R. F., and Mullins, D. W. "The Gains to Bidding Firms from Merger." *Journal of Financial Economics* (January-February 1986), pp. 121–39.

Alexander, G. J., Benson, P. G., and Kampmeyer, J. M. "Investigating the Valuation Effects of Announcements of Voluntary Corporate Selloffs." *Journal of Finance* (June 1984), pp. 503–17.

Boudreaux, K. "Divestiture and Share Price." *Journal of Financial and Quantitative Analysis* (November 1975), pp. 619–26.

Bradley, M. "Interfirm Offers and the Market for Corporate Control." *Journal of Business* (October 1980), pp. 183–206.

"Buying Out to Avoid a Takeover." *Business Week,* May 14, 1979, p. 115.

Dann, L. Y., and DeAngelo, H. "Standstill Agreements, Privately Negotiated

Stock Repurchases, and the Market for Corporate Control." *Journal of Financial Economics* (November 1983), pp. 274–300.

DeAngelo, H., DeAngelo, L., and Rice, E. M. "Going Private." *Journal of Law and Economics* (October 1984), pp. 367–401.

Dennis, D. K., and McConnell, J. "Corporate Mergers and Security Returns." *Journal of Financial Economics* (June 1980), pp. 143–87.

Dodd, P. R. "Merger Proposals, Management Discretion and Stockholder Wealth." *Journal of Financial Economics* (June 1980), pp. 105–37.

Flaherty, R. J., and Greene, R. "Oxy vs. Mead." *Forbes* (December 11, 1978), pp. 45–50.

Goff, N. "Takeover Backlash." *Financial World* (June 15, 1979), pp. 15–20.

Hite, G. L., and Owers, J. E. "Security Price Reactions around Corporate Spin-Off Announcements." *Journal of Financial Economics* (December 1983), pp. 409–36.

Jain, P. C. "The Effect of Voluntary Sell-off Announcements on Shareholder Wealth." *The Journal of Finance* (March 1985), pp. 209–24.

Jensen, M. C., and Ruback, R. S. "The Market for Corporate Control." *Journal of Financial Economics* (April 1983), pp. 5–50.

Klein, April. "The Timing and Substance of Divestiture Announcements." *The Journal of Finance* (July 1986), pp. 685–97.

Kolbenschlag, M. "Digging In." *Forbes* (August 4, 1980), pp. 37–38.

Linn, S. C., and McConnell, J. J. "An Empirical Investigation of the Impact of Antitakeover Amendments on Common Stock Prices." *Journal of Financial Economics* (April 1983), pp. 361–400.

Miles, J. A., and Rosenfeld, J. D. "The Effect of Voluntary Spin-off Announcements on Shareholder Wealth." *Journal of Finance* (December 1983), pp. 1597–1606.

"A New Ploy to Fight Takeovers." *Business Week,* May 24, 1982, p. 91.

Rosenfeld, J. D. "Additional Evidence on the Relation between Divestiture Announcements and Shareholder Wealth." *Journal of Finance* (December 1984), pp. 1437–447.

Skantz, T. R., and Marchesini, R. "The Effect of Voluntary Corporate Liquidation on Shareholder Wealth." *Journal of Financial Research* (Spring 1987), pp. 65–75.

Tehranian, H., Travlos, N. G., and Waegelein, J. F. "The Effect of Long-Term Performance Plans on Corporate Sell-Off-Induced Abnormal Returns." *Journal of Finance* (September 1987), pp. 933–41.

10

Miscellaneous Corporate Events

Any number of corporate events might affect a company's common stock, among them strikes, investigations, and accidents. Many have been studied and their impact documented.

STRIKES

In recent years, strikes have become increasingly bitter. Violent rhetoric and sometimes even violent actions occur during the course of strikes. Some researchers, like Eaton (1972) and Imberman (1979), conclude that strikes are bad investments for a corporation. Using event methodology, however, Davidson et al. (1988) examined the impact of strike activity on 240 companies from 1978–83 and found significant reaction to the announcement of a strike. They also found that there is a negative drift, although statistically insignificant, in residuals during the 30 days prior to a strike announcement, and that the negative returns for strikes are greater for longer strikes than shorter ones. The authors conclude that the market anticipates which strikes will be longer, and prices accordingly.

RATINGS CHANGES

Several researchers have examined stock behavior surrounding announcements of changes in corporate security ratings by various rating agencies. The timing of the impact appears to be of interest in these studies.

For instance Glascock et al. (1987) examined stock return behavior surrounding the announcement of bond rating changes by Moody's Bond Service. They report a downward drift before the announcement of a downgrading of a bond, indicating that the market noted disturbing factors pertaining to the company and discounted the stock accordingly. This in turn affected the financial health of the company and caused the bond rating agency to reassess the company's credibility. However, they do note a significant impact on the publication date of the Moody's Bond Survey, rather than on the day the rerating announcement was made. The authors conclude that the market is therefore somewhat slow to assimilate rerating information. They note that this is somewhat puzzling, in view of the downward drift in stock prices prior to the announcement date. This inconsistency is not explained.

Stickel (1986) examined preferred stock rating changes on preferred and common stock prices and found an impact on preferred prices the day after announcement. They found no evidence, however, of an impact on common stock prices.

DEBT SWAPS

Peavy and Scott (1985) examined stock for debt swaps and resulting impact on stockholder and bondholder wealth, and found a significant negative impact on stockholder wealth, but no perceptible effect on bondholder wealth.

CORPORATE CAPITAL EXPENDITURES

McConnell and Muscarella (1985), using event methodology, examined 658 corporations around the dates when they announced future capital expenditure plans. They found that announcements of increases in planned capital expenditures resulted in significant positive returns.

Conversely, when companies announced cuts in planned capital expenditures, negative excess stock returns resulted.

AIRLINE CRASHES

Barrett et al. (1987) used event study in gauging the impact of fatal commercial airline crashes on the stocks of airline companies, and found that the negative impact of a fatal crash is significant for only one full trading day after the event.

PRODUCT RECALLS

In an interesting study, Jarrell and Peltzman (1985) showed what happens to stockholder wealth surrounding product recalls. They examined drug companies and automobile manufacturers who had to recall defective products from the market and found that shareholders bore large losses—losses greater than the costs that could be traced directly to the recall, such as repairing the defective product. They found the impact spilled over even to competitors. In other words, recalls must raise serious doubts about the overall value of a company, and even an industry.

RECOMMENDATIONS AND OPINIONS

Certain advisory firms and investment firms may have an impact on the perceived value of stocks. Peterson (1987) studied the impact of Value Line Investment Advisory Surveys on stock price and found significant abnormal returns for the three-day period surrounding the publication date. The significant returns were for portfolios consisting of securities ranked days one, two, and four.

Glascock et al. (1986) found that when E. F. Hutton talks, people really do listen. They studied securities recommended by E. F. Hutton and found that recommended stocks perform well. Further, strongly recommended securities performed better than less vigorously recommended securities.

Dopuch et al. (1986) examined stock returns associated with announcements of "subject to" qualified audit opinions. For the 109 observations studied, they reported an average abnormal return of -4.7 percent for the three-day period surrounding the announcement date.

INDEXES AND EXCHANGES

Lamoureux and Wansley (1987) examined the impact on stock price of firms either deleted from or added to the Standard and Poor's 500 index. They found that, after 1975, firms added to the index experienced a significant positive announcement-day effect. Deleted firms had significant negative returns. This effect for changes prior to 1975 does not exist, however.

The value of a listing on the New York Stock Exchange was studied by Grammatikos and Papaioannou (1986), who found that listings had an impact on firms that performed differently in the prelisting period. They found that companies with high earnings performance prior to announcement showed market reaction. On the other hand, firms that had low earnings performance had a positive price reaction during the announcement period, but a negative price reaction after the listing.

INVESTIGATION AND CRIME

The popular television program *60 Minutes* reaches the masses. Its popularity results from the cutting edge of its investigative journalism. Occasionally, these investigations focus on corporations. Davidson et al. (1985) studied the impact of *60 Minutes* stories on stock prices. Surprisingly, they found that after stories were aired, stock prices of firms covered in the investigations went up, not down.

Strachan et al. (1983) report the effect that announcements of alleged corporate crime have on common stock market value. Firms involved in such scandals, they purport, have a statistically significant loss in market value.

FINANCIAL INSTITUTIONS

In an interesting study, Hatfield and Lancaster (1989) report on the changing environment in which financial institutions operate. Their study is included in an appendix to this chapter.

CONCLUSION

All the events covered in this book affect shareholder wealth. Sometimes, the impact is not what would normally be expected. A shrewd investor can study corporate events and use such knowledge for financial gain. Managers can use such knowledge to avert financial disaster for their company. One caution must be kept in mind, however: just because an event affected a stock price in a certain way in the past does not mean the impact will always be the same. Things change.

REFERENCES

Barrett, W. B., Heuson, A. J., Kolb, R. W., and Schropp, G. H. "The Adjustment of Stock Prices to Completely Unanticipated Events." *The Financial Review* (November 1987), pp. 345–54.

Davidson, W. N., Chandy, P. R., and Garrison, S. H. "A Short Note on the Effect of Broadcasting on Stock Returns." *Journal of Portfolio Management* (Winter 1985), pp. 23–27.

Davidson, W. N., Garrison, S. H., and Worrell, D. R. "The Effect of Strike Activity on Firm Value." *Academy of Management Journal* (June 1988), pp. 67–87.

Dopuch, N., Holthausen, R. W., and Leftwich, R. W. "Abnormal Stock Returns Associated with Media Disclosures of 'Subject to' Qualified Audit Opinions." *Journal of Accounting and Economics* 8 (1986), pp. 93–117.

Eaton, B. C. "The Worker and the Profitability of the Strike." *Industrial and Labor Relations Review* (October 1972), pp. 26–28.

Glascock, J. L., Davidson, W. N., and Henderson, G. V. "Announcement Effects of Moody's Bond Rating Changes." *Quarterly Journal of Business and Economics* (Summer 1987), pp. 67–79.

Glascock, J. L., Henderson, G. V., and Martin, L. J. "When E. F. Hutton Talks . . ." *Financial Analysts Journal* (May–June 1986), pp. 69–72.

Grammatikos, T., and Papaioannou, G. J. "The Informational Value of Listing on the New York Stock Exchange." *The Financial Review* (November 1986), pp. 485–98.

Hatfield, G., and Lancaster, C. "Announcement Effects On Bank Stock Prices: Citicorp's Increase in Loan Loss Reserves for Third World Debt." *Journal of Financial and Strategic Decisions* 2, no. 3 (1989).

Imberman, W. "Strikes Cost More Than You Think." *Harvard Business Review* (May–June 1979), pp. 56–58.

Jarrell, G., and Peltzman, S. "The Impact of Product Recalls on the Wealth of Sellers." *Journal of Political Economy* 93, no. 3 (June 1985), pp. 512–36.

Lamoureux, C. G., and Wansley, J. W. "Market Effects of Changes in the Standard & Poor's 500 Index." *The Financial Review* (February 1987), pp. 53–69.

Peavy, J. W., and Scott, J. A. "The Effect of Stock for Debt Swaps on Security Returns." *The Financial Review* (November 1985), pp. 303–27.

Peterson, David. "Security Price Reactions to Initial Reviews of Common Stock by the Value Line Investment Survey." *Journal of Financial and Quantitative Analysis* (December 1987), pp. 483–94.

Stickel, S. "The Effect of Preferred Stock Rating Changes on Preferred and Common Stock Prices." *Journal of Accounting and Economics* 8 (1986), pp. 197–215.

Strachan, S. L., Smith, D. B., and Beedles, W. L. "The Price Reaction to Alleged Corporate Crime." *The Financial Review* (May 1983), pp. 121–32.

Appendix 10.1: Announcement Effects on Bank Stock Prices: Citicorp's Increase in Loan Loss Reserves for Third World Debt

INTRODUCTION

Citicorp's announcement of a sizeable increase to its loan loss reserve account was a landmark public admission of possible loan default by third world debtor nations. This paper analyzes the impact of the announcement on Citicorp, the banking industry, and the stock market. The results provide evidence of a positive response to Citicorp's action. There is additional evidence that the size of the market response is related to an individual bank's degree of international loan exposure.

On May 19, 1987, Citicorp's chair, John Reed, publicly announced that the bank was increasing, effective immediately, its loan loss reserves by $3 billion in order to cushion the bank's loan exposure against possible default by financially unstable third world countries. Total foreign debt owed by the Baker Plan countries was $437 billion, with $62 billion of it owed to the United States financial community. The tradition in the banking industry had been to renegotiate, stretch out payments, and lower interest rates. Reed's announcement not only broke this tradition but was also the first public admission that the loans were worth less than their face value.

The purpose of this chapter is to determine whether there was a reaction in the market, either to Citicorp or the banking industry, as a result of this announcement. A positive reaction might occur because the market approves the recognition of these problem loans; on the other hand, no significant reaction could be explained by the fact that additions to reserves are primarily accounting transactions. The possible relationship between the size of investor response and the degree of international loan exposure is also analyzed. The paper is arranged into sections as follows: background of the international loan problem and Reed's announcement, data and methodology, and results and conclusions.

This appendix is reprinted from Gay B. Hatfield and Carol Lancaster, "Announcement Effects on Bank Stock Prices: Citicorp's Increase in Loan Loss Reserves for Third World Debt," *Journal of Financial and Strategic Decisions* 2, no. 3, 1989.

BACKGROUND

The debt crisis was initiated in August, 1982, when Mexico declared a moratorium on its foreign debt payments and almost defaulted on loans worth $82 billion. Since 1983, only Colombia and Venezuela have made any principal payments. In February, 1987, when Brazil announced it would only pay interest to public creditors, such as the International Monetary Fund and World Bank, major banks retaliated by classifying the Brazilian loans as nonperforming (Fierman, 1987). Talks concerning debt rescheduling were planned for June.

On Tuesday, May 19, 1987, John Reed held a press conference at which he announced Citicorp's intention to immediately add $3 billion to its loan loss reserves to cover possible international loan losses. This was the public announcement; however, because of the possible tremors that could result from the announcement, Reed had conferred with the Federal Reserve Board, the Securities and Exchange Commission, James Baker and the Treasury Department, and the rating agencies. Consequently, rumors of the pending announcement were circulating in the stock and bond markets several days before the actual date of the press conference. Despite leaking information, the bank's decision still appeared to have a stunning effect. The Dow Jones Industrial Average and the New York Index both declined the day of the announcement; however, the market stabilized and the indexes climbed back up. By the end of the week, the price of Citicorp's common stock had risen by five dollars.

Three studies (Cornell and Shapiro, 1986; Bruner and Simms, 1987; and Glascock et al., 1987) analyzed the market reaction to the debt crisis of 1982. Cornell and Shapiro (1986), using cross-sectional regression analysis, concluded that, over the period from 1982 to 1983, foreign loan exposure did affect the prices of bank stocks, but that this reaction was continually impounded in the stock prices.

Bruner and Simms (1987) stated that Cornell and Shapiro (1986) did not answer the question as to how rapidly the market reacted to the Mexican debt moratorium. They tested two hypotheses. First, any new information concerning deterioration "will be quickly impounded in the share prices of the affected banks." Second, the size of the response will be directly related to the size of each bank's foreign debt exposure. Since the authors were specifically interested in measuring the effect of the Mexican debt moratorium, they selected August 19,

1982, as the event date and used standard event study methodology. They found that the announcement did convey new information concerning the Mexican loans, and that the news was impounded in the share price of banks with this exposure. Furthermore, they found that it took the market six days to impound the news, whereas Cornell and Shapiro (1986) concluded that the impounding took four months. In addition, they found that the size of the response was related to the size of exposure, but only after five days or more. They concluded that it took investors several days to discover an individual bank's exposure.

Glascock et al. (1987) investigated whether international default affected the equity returns of all banks and found multinational banks and regional wholesale banks had significant negative returns on the event day, while regional consumer banks did not. Consequently, not all bank stock returns were affected.

DATA AND METHODOLOGY

The sample selected for this study includes Citicorp and five other banks, including Chemical New York, Bankers Trust New York, First Chicago, First Interstate Bancorporation, and Marine Midland. Because the intent is to measure the market's reaction to Citicorp's announcement, the additional banks chosen had to be those that did not immediately follow Citicorp's lead and add to their loan loss reserves. In addition, the banks needed to have substantial international loan exposure and be listed on the New York Stock Exchange. The sample period was from December 1, 1986, to June 10, 1987. Daily security stock price data was hand collected for calculating returns from individual issues of the *Wall Street Journal* and covered one hundred days prior to the test period and fifteen days on either side of the announcement date.

The following is an abbreviated discussion of the statistical procedure, as is often presented by others (see Davidson et al., 1989); for a more detailed description of event time methodology, see the appendix to Dodd and Warner (1983).

To test the market's reaction to the announcement of Citicorp's increase in loan loss reserves, the single-index market model was used to predict returns:

$$R_{jt} = \alpha_j + \beta_j R_{mt} + e_{jt} \qquad \text{(Eq. 1)}$$

where

R_{jt} = rate of return on security j for day t

R_{mt} = rate of return on the New York Stock Exchange Index on day t

α_j = ordinary least squares estimate of the intercept (constant term) from regression

β_j = ordinary least squares estimate of the slope from regression.

The parameter estimates are from preevent data. The prediction error (PE_{jt}) (excess return) for security j and event day t is computed for the forecast period as follows:

$$PE_{jt} = R_{jt} - (\hat{\alpha}_j + \hat{\beta}_j R_{mt}) \qquad \text{(Eq. 2)}$$

Prediction errors are calculated for each security over the interval $t = -15$ to $t = 15$, relative to the event day. The Cumulative Prediction Error (CPE_j) over various intervals T_{1j} to T_{2j} is calculated as follows:

$$CPE_j = \sum_{t=T_{1j}}^{T_{2j}} PE_{jt} \qquad \text{(Eq. 3)}$$

The mean cumulative prediction error, for a sample of N securities, is defined as follows:

$$\overline{CPE} = \frac{1}{N} \sum_{j=1}^{N} CPE_j \qquad \text{(Eq. 4)}$$

In the absence of abnormal performance, the expected value of the $\overline{CPE}$ is zero. The test statistic, described by Dodd and Warner (1983), is based on an aggregation of mean standardized CPEs. The PE_{jt} are standardized by their estimated standard deviations s_{jt} as follows:

$$SPE_{jt} = PE_{jt} \div s_{jt} \qquad \text{(Eq. 5)}$$

The standard deviation s_{jt} is adjusted for each observation's distance away from the mean of the independent variable and is directly associated with the time series standard deviation for each firm. Due to the normal variation for different firms, the same size prediction error may have different levels of significance for different firms.

The standardized CPE ($SCPE_j$) over the interval $t = T_{1j} \ldots T_{2j}$ is:

$$\overline{SCPE_j} = \sum_{t=T_{1j}}^{T_{2j}} SPE_{jt} \div \sqrt{T_{2j} - T_{1j} + 1} \qquad \text{(Eq. 6)}$$

The test statistic for a sample of N securities is:

$$Z(CPE) = \sum_{j=1}^{N} \overline{SCPE_j} \div \sqrt{N} \qquad \text{(Eq. 7)}$$

In the absence of abnormal performance, each SPE_{jt} is assumed to be distributed unit normal; therefore, with this assumption, $Z(CPE)$ is also unit normal.

The event date for this study is May 19, 1987, the day of the Citicorp press conference.

RESULTS

Table 10.1 (section A), shows the CPEs and associated test statistics for several different intervals within the test period on a sample of all six banks. Several of the intervals are noteworthy. The entire test interval, day -15 to $+15$, has a CPE of .087 ($Z = 2.715$), demonstrating an overall positive drift in residuals, or excess returns, of 8.7 percent for the bank stocks over the length of the test period.

The interval -15 to -6 is statistically significant with a CPE of .049 ($Z = 2.784$). Much of the reaction within this time period may be traced to an even stronger reaction in the interval -11 to -9 ($CPE = 0.032$, $Z = 3.311$). There are two possible explanations. The *Wall Street Journal* carried an article on May 4 (day -11) announcing boosts in first-quarter profits for big banks trading in currencies (Truell

Table 10.1
Cumulative Prediction Error Results for Announcement Effect of Citicorp's Increase in Loan Loss Reserves for Third World Debt on May 19, 1987 [c]

Interval		(A) With Citicorp		(B) Without Citicorp	
		CPE	Z(CPE)	CPE	Z(CPE)
-15	15	0.0866	2.7152[a]	0.0749	2.1547[b]
-15	- 6	0.0491	2.7839[a]	0.0517	2.6960[a]
-11	- 9	0.0324	3.3115[a]	0.0301	2.8284[a]
-10	- 1	-0.0007	0.0233	0.0094	0.5331
- 5	- 1	-0.0202	-1.6143	-0.0156	-1.1672
- 1	0	-0.0017	-0.2010	-0.0018	-0.2110
0	0	-0.0030	-0.5817	-0.0079	-1.3200
0	1	-0.0087	-1.0138	-0.0120	-1.2995
1	15	0.0607	2.7126[a]	0.0467	1.9111
2	3	0.0224	2.5756[a]	0.0065	0.5485
2	15	0.0664	3.0355[a]	0.0508	2.1165[b]

[a]Significant at the .01 level.

[b]Significant at the .05 level.

[c]We have shown the cumulative prediction errors and associated test statistics for representative intervals across the forecast period, t=-15 to t=15, relative to the event date of May 19, 1987. Column A includes the results for all six banks in the study. In order to determine the impact of Citicorp itself on the results in Column A, we ran a second sample excluding Citicorp. The results of the second sample are presented in Column B. It would appear that the only major difference between results from the two samples involves the statistically significant reaction of Citicorp stock on days +2 and +3, a reaction obviously not felt, at least to the same extent, by the other five banks as a group.

and Guenther, 1987), with five of the six banks from this study being listed in the article. Two other *Wall Street Journal* articles indicated other possible explanations: one article (on May 5, day −10) reported the previous day's announcement of a reorganization of the World

Bank in an attempt to broaden its role in managing third world debt (Stevens, 1979); the second article (on May 6, day −9) reported an overall surge in stock prices on the previous day in reaction to a stronger bond market and a stronger dollar (Lacrica, 1987).

The short intervals leading up to and including the event day (May 19) are primarily negative and statistically insignificant. A reversal of signs and a strong positive drift can be seen in the CPEs from day +2 through the end of the test period (CPE = 0.066, Z = 3.036). These findings indicate that the information was indeed a positive signal to the market, apparently fueled by a statistically significant reaction to two announcements on days +2 and +3 (CPE = 0.022, Z = 2.576). On day +2 (May 21) the *Wall Street Journal* carried an article predicting that other big U.S. banks would follow Citicorp's example and increase their loan reserves for third world debt (Truell and Guenther, 1987). On day +3 (May 22) the *Wall Street Journal* reported Citicorp's plan to cut loans to debtor nations by approximately $5 billion over the next three years. The report also outlined Citicorp's strategy for accomplishing the cuts through debt-for-equity swaps and sales (Truell and Guenther). It would appear that the market had previously taken a wait and see attitude following Reed's original announcement. The additional information released on May 21–22 was apparently the confirmation the market needed to react with confidence.

In order to determine the impact of Citicorp on results from the first sample, a separate sample excluding Citicorp was examined. Although including Citicorp increased the magnitude of the test statistics in those intervals discussed above, there was only one statistically different interval (see Table 10.1, section B). The statistically significant +2 to +3 interval from the complete sample (CPE = 0.022, Z = 2.576) appears to be predominantly influenced by Citicorp. The corresponding interval in the sample without Citicorp has a CPE of 0.006 (Z = 0.549). It is, however, interesting to note that the three banks in this study having the largest Latin American exposure each had a statistically significant PE on day +3 (Z > 2.0), while none of the banks with less than $3 billion in loans showed a statistically significant reaction on this day (see Table 10.2). This appears to be consistent with Bruner and Simms's (1987) conclusion that size of investor response is related to degree of exposure of each bank. Glascock et al. (1987) also found that international defaults do not affect all bank stock returns.

Table 10.2

Amount of Latin American Loan Exposure of Individual Sample Banks and the Degree of Investor Response

Bank	$ Amount of Loans (in billions)[a]	PE (Daily t) (Day +3)
Citicorp	11.7	.048 (3.343)[b]
Chemical New York	5.3	.033 (2.625)[c]
Bankers Trust New York	3.2	.033 (2.065)[c]
First Chicago	2.6	.006 (0.456)
Marine Midland	1.8	-.008 (-0.684)
First Interstate Bancorp	1.5	.002 (0.160)

[a]Source: *The Wall Street Journal*, June 8, 1987, p. 6.

[b]Significant at the .01 level.

[c]Significant at the .05 level.

CONCLUSIONS

For the single event date of May 19, 1987, there was found no significant reaction in bank stock prices to the announcement that Citicorp had added $3 billion to its reserves against losses on loans to third world countries. However, as expected, there was an overall positive trend in residuals across the test period. It is likely that Reed's preparations prior to the announcement did not go unnoticed, making it probable that the information was impounded in the stock price of Citicorp long before the public announcement. This may help explain the statistically significant CPEs during the first week of the test period.

Furthermore, the market demonstrated a surge of confidence, as indicated by a strong positive drift beginning two days after the event day. Our finding is similar to the delay found by Bruner and Simms

(1987), indicating that the market may need a few days to determine which banks will be affected by the new information. Also in agreement with Bruner and Simms's study, there is evidence that the size of investor response is related to the degree of exposure of each bank.

Due to the single event date for all banks in this study, the findings may suffer from a clustering problem. The decline of both the Dow Jones Industrial Average and the New York Index on the announcement day may indicate a marketwide reaction, which can mask individual effects on the banks in this study. Further research should be done to test the results using a two-beta model to adjust for industry effects that may cause a bias in studies such as this one.

REFERENCES

"BankAmerica Raising Reserve $1.1 Billion; Manufacturers Hanover Mulls Similar Step." *Wall Street Journal* (June 1987), p. 3.

Bartlett, Sarah. "A Stunner from the Citi." *Business Week* (June 1987), pp. 42–43.

Berton, Lee. "Auditors Press Banks to Bite Bullet on Foreign Loans." *Wall Street Journal* (June 1987), p. 6.

Bruner, Robert F., and Simms, John M., Jr. "The International Debt Crisis and Bank Security Returns in 1982." *Journal of Money, Credit, and Banking* (February 1987), p. 46–55.

Cornell, Bradford, and Shapiro, Alan C. "The Reaction of Bank Stock Prices to the International Debt Crisis." *Journal of Banking and Finance* 10 (1986), pp. 57–73.

Davidson, Wallace N., Dutia, Dipa, and Cheng, Louis. "A Re-examination of the Market Reaction to Failed Mergers." *The Journal of Finance* (September 1989), pp. 1077–1083.

Dodd, P., and Warner, J. "On Corporate Governance: A Study of Proxy Contests." *Journal of Financial Economics* (April 1983), pp. 401–438.

"Facing Up to Reality, Citicorp Adds $3 Billion to Loan Loss Reserves." *Wall Street Journal* (May 1987), p. 1.

Fierman, Jaclyn. "John Reed's Bold Stroke." *Fortune* (June 22, 1987), pp. 26–32.

Glascock, John L., Karafiath, Imre, and Strand, Robert W. "The Effect of the International Debt Crisis on U.S. Bank Equity Returns." Working Paper, October 1987.

Herman, Tom, and Sesit, Michael R. "Bond Prices Rise as U.S. Begins Refunding Sales." *Wall Street Journal* (May 6, 1987), p. 3.

Koepp, Stephen. "Citicorp Breaks Ranks." *Time* (June 1, 1987), pp. 48–50.

Lacrica, Eduardo. "World Bank Sets Revamping to Widen Role in Managing Debt in Third World." *Wall Street Journal* (May 5, 1987), p. 5.

Pauly, David, Friday, Carolyn, and Thomas, Rich. "Citicorp Faces Reality—and Finds It Doesn't Hurt." *Newsweek* (June 1, 1987), pp. 42–45.

Stevens, Charles W. "Big Banks Gain from Trading in Currencies." *Wall Street Journal* (May 4, 1987), p. 44.

Truell, Peter. "Citicorp Plans to Shed Big Part of Loans to Third World through Swaps, Sales." *Wall Street Journal* (May 22, 1987), p. 2.

Truell, Peter, and Guenther, Robert. "Big U.S. Banks Seen Boosting Loan Reserves." *Wall Street Journal* (May 21, 1987), p. 2.

Index

About the Author

SHARON H. GARRISON is Associate Professor of Finance at East Tennessee State University and Editor of *The Journal of Financial and Strategic Decisions*. She is co-author of *Financial Forecasting and Planning* (Quorum, 1988).